Reprinted from the Gazette, Berkeley, California

Technocracy

PART I.

Human Instincts in Reconstruction.
An Analysis of Urges and a Suggestion For Their Direction.

By William Henry Smyth

Note—The author shows that the forces of the four great human instincts—to live, to make, to take, to control—are as essential in modern social life as at any time in the past. But all of these urges in a living democracy should be controlled without being controlled. To achieve this seeming paradox we must have a great national purpose, and unselfish leadership such as could come through a National Council of Scientists.

Mr. William Henry Smyth has been in general practice as a consulting engineer since 1879. He is the inventor of many machines and mechanical devices, including a system of raising water by direct explosion on its surface, the device being known as the "direct explosion pump." He has been an engineering expert in many patent cases, and is a frequent contributor to technical journals. As well as a pioneer in mechanics, Mr. Smyth is a pioneer in economics. He is a member of the leading scholarly associations in that field, including the American Economic Association and the Royal Economic Society of Great Britain.

Parts I, II and III appeared originally in "Industrial Management" of New York. The concluding Part IV has not heretofore been published and will appear exclusively in The Gazette.—Editor.

Instincts Control.

Instincts are the most persistent human urge factors. Seemingly, they are less subject to change than even the most unchanging aspects of our physical environment.

The Instinct to Live (self-preservation) is as dominating today as in the days of our cave-man ancestors; the Instinct to Construct is as persistent in Man as in the beaver; the Mastery Instinct (desire to control others) is as vital as ever; the Thievish Instinct (desire to acquire and hoard) shows no change, and is the same old urge as that disclosed by the pre-man stores of insects, birds and various animals.

Indeed, without these primordial urges Man could not have developed, and the loss or atrophy of any one of them would probably mean the rapid extinction of the race. Thus it would seem that our fundamental instincts are essentially necessary to human continuance—at least, to our social existence. So let us look once more at these vital factors, in the light of recent events, in order to see what part they now take and are likely to play in our future social economy.

Brute Force.

No lesson of the war, probably, is more obvious or more clearly defined than the rapid trend toward Skill as a predominating and controlling factor in our immediate social development.

Recorded history and archaeological investigation confirm the suggestion that in the matter of economic control of human activities and their products, the possession of this control has oscillated to and fro under the influence of one or other of the instinctive urges, so that characteristic types of men secured alternate mastery.

Starting in the pre-human period, before the dawn of definite self-consciousness, and continuing during eons in the twilight of human intelligence, raw brute force must have been the dominating economic factor.

The influence of Skill during this period was practically negligible, except in so far as it affected individuals. Of this the huge prolongation of the unchanging "Stone Age" is sufficient demonstration.

Contest With Cunning.

The gradual growth and rapid culmination of the Skill factor is an important consideration in our present inquiry and likewise in our Social Reconstruction problems. For while Purposive Skill is of slow development Purposive Cunning, on the contrary, is inherently otherwise. Indeed, Cunning and Purposiveness both imply mental alertness and hence are in some wise synonymous.

For these reasons, in the early stages of human development, raw strength and animal cunning must alone have contended to satisfy the other instinctive urges—to live, to control—practically uninfluenced by the relatively modern urge of Purposeful Skill.

Doubtless this simple conflict (of raw strength and brute cunning) waged with varying results, slowly oscillating, age by age and race by race, in favor of one or other human type as environmental conditions or racial admixtures gave one or other the advantage of circumstance.

And, as Economics implies: the usages, laws, and institutions whereby a community endeavors to organize its methods and means of living: those whose activities characterize the times initiate and administer its economics.

Age-Long See-Saw.

So, with these age-long oscillations of control types, economic institutions necessarily underwent like changes. conforming to the dominating human characteristics of each Age and Nation. That they did so oscillate and economically conform, in the vaguest dawn of human beginnings, is the teaching of archaeology.

During the past few thousand years the contest of Strength and Cunning is shown by reliable historical records to have oscillated with comparative · rapidity between one and the other extreme—including considerable periods during which Strength and Cunning unified control by union of Church and State.

Prior to the immediate present was a transition stage caused by the gradual weakening of the bond between Church and State, with a coincidental shifting of control in favor of Cunning (under a changed and relatively modern guise representing the instinctive Urge to Take) expressing itself as Commercialism. With this change came a consequent modification of usages, laws, and institutions appropriate to its highest expression—Capitalism—capitalistic economics. The result of this last oscillation of control in favor of (acquisitive) Cunning was that Germany became a nation of slaves, England a nation of paupers, France quit breeding, and the United States went wealth crazy!

Challenge by Purposive Skill.

The war represents the conclusive termination (in this period) of the age-long contest of Force and Cunning—for the control of men, and the products of their activity.

But this last and most spectacular conflict is complicated by the intrusion of the most modern and most rapidly developing factor—Organized Purposive Skill.

Here, then, Skill enters the arena with a challenge to both earlier contestants—for the prize of human control, and mastery of the social machinery; enters that contest—older than the race itself—the struggle to satisfy the primordial instincts: to Live—to Control—to Take.

Strength vs. Cunning vs. Skill.

Thus the contest has become a triangular fight between the Strong, the Cunning, and the Skilful; a fight in which raw brute force is a participant of rapidly diminishing importance—a modified continuation of the old time bloody contest, for a humanly undesirable outcome.

Cunning-control is today the victor, and in possession of the spoils—the financial wealth of the world. But all the evidence points to a short enjoyment and a losing fight against the organized forces of Purposeful Skill.

Creaking Capitalism Cracking.

Capitalism—under war stress—shows convincing evidence of inadequacy. The non-effectiveness of money and credit wealth has become so obvious as to procure the enactment of "Work or Fight" laws. Thus, into the discard went our prewar money evaluation of men to be substituted by a standard which measures millionaire and hobo alike in accordance with their relative skill.

Our pre-war faith in the mysterious Magic of Money too received a staggering shock when all the private fortunes enmassed and all the billions of national credit combined utterly failed to add a single pound of much needed sugar to our limited supply, necessitating the "two pounds of sugar per person" apportionment—a commonplace vulgar fraction measure applicable to Financial Potentate and Weary Willie—alike!

Producer Versus Parasite.

On broader lines also the evidence points the same way: purposive skill is inherently productive, while purposeful cunning is naturally parasitic. Then, the capability of cunning to rule, and the continuance of its success in controlling others, resides in and depends upon the stupidity and illiteracy of the governed: mystery and magic are its weapons—equally in the realm of modern Finance as in the ancient Theocracies.

Skill implies the reverse of all this, for skill is intelligence physically manifested. It is knowledge of Nature's Laws utilized dexterously—and the spread of scientific information characterizes our age. Thus as the bulwarks of cunning-control crumble, the weapons of skill are multiplied and perfected.

So the outcome seems a foregone conclusion.

With this outcome, our methods of life will necessarily change. Capitalistic customs, laws, and institutions will be substituted by others differing as widely from those with which we are familiar as the motor ideas and ideals of purposeful cunning differ from those of purposeful skill.

"Work or Fight" Lesson.

Peradventure, the "Work or Fight" and the "2 pounds of sugar per person" measures are tonic foretastes of the coming Skill-Economics.

Obviously we are in transition to a new social order.

The signs of the times portend the dethroning of decadent acquisitive capitalism and the crowning of productive skill—Autocrat of the new Age—Artizanism.

This change has been in dubious process for years; the War has merely speeded its progress and made the outcome practically inevitable. But, whether it be brought about by evolution or revolution, or whether it comes in clean-cut aspect or befogged by irrelevant social factors and forces, it is in no sense a rational or final solution of our "social problem."

In any event, should Artizanism come, it will be merely another social spasm, probably shorter than, but equally as futile as, our present worldwide finance madness.

Instincts Not A Rational Basis.

While it is conceivable that human societies could be organized upon and with any one of the stated basic Instincts as dominant factor and raison d'etre; it is practically certain that any such national society would be quite ineffective, and transient. For obviously it would not and could not satisfy even our present limited intelligence, our rational imagination, or our modern spiritual ideals.

No very extended analysis would be required to show the validity of this proposition. The past has already demonstrated the insufficiency of societies based upon the Mastery Instinct—Autocracy. The present amply proves the failure of the Acquisitive Instinct as a social basis—Plutocracy.

A moment's thought will show that a society based upon the Making Instinct would simply crumble in its formative process under the demands of our complicated modern mental make-up, for clearly this instinct provides inadequate Human scope—and hence presupposes parasitism in even more extended form than that of acquisitive Capitalism. And — worse than all—a society based upon the Instinct to Live and Propagate, would return us at once to the brute state from which we have arisen through ages of struggle, strife, and bloodshed.

Control Without Control.

Still, it is apparent that the basic instincts which urge "to live," "to make," "to take," "to control," are as useful, yes, are as essential in and to modern social life as they have been in all the past. But, while all are necessary, no one of them constitutes a proper basis—law of operation—for a rational human society organization. They are factors, necessary and desirable contributary parts, no one of which is inherently adapted to function as the machine's unifier, its strain and speed equalizer—its control element.

Thus, the determination of a suitable character of "control" element is seemingly the crux of our social problem; the problem of controlling without control, that old, old paradox: Freedom made effective by restraint— a paradox, however, which the war may have resolved for us, by demonstrating its non-existence.

It has, in somewise, answered our troublous question by clear definition in the statement of the Nation's object in going to war.

The war has answered the question, in another aspect, by the Nation's adoption of the method (forced upon it by logical compulsion) whereby success was achieved.

"To make the World safe for Democracy" is the clearest and most universally accepted statement of our purpose in going to war—Self-government for Nations, Self-government for Individuals.

Concept of Control.

Control by others, then, is antithetical to the ideals for which we have waged this last, the greatest, and, it is hoped, the final bloody contest for Self-government.

Control is equally antithetical to our Ideals of Self-government whether the control is exercised by "others" characterized by the Instinct to live and breed—the Masses; or whether the control is exercised by "others" characterized by the Instinct to Make— the Skilled Artizan; or whether the control is exercised by "others" urged by the Instinct of Mastery—the Employers; or whether the control is exercised by "others" under their dominating Acquisitive Instinct — the Financiers.

Indeed, the concept: control by "others," is an idea inherent in and appropriate only to now discredited Autocracy—a concept which the War has rendered an obsolete ideal—if we are yet intelligent enough to profit by its costly teaching.

Discard Cave-Man Control.

To be rationally consistent this "control" concept should be as absent as it is obsolete (in fact and effect) in our inevitable reconstruction.

This Autocracy "control" concept must be thrown in the discard where we have dumped the European autocrats whose ideal it was—if our reconstruction efforts are intended to produce a rationally organized Modern Human Society; a Society founded upon the Ideals consecrated by the life blood of our bravest and best.

But our age-long familiarity with "control by others," in our halting progress, from brute beast to modern Man, has so deeply ingrained in our mental fiber this stone-age concept as to make it almost impossible for us to even conceive the idea of a society lacking this cave-man spiked-club element.

Yet, no fact and lesson of our participation in the War is more clear and free from doubt than the spontaneous acquiescence by the people of the United States—rich and poor, artizan and laborer, alike—in self-control, self-repression, self-dedication to the united will and unified purpose of the Nation.

Purpose.

No lesson of the War is more significant than: Given a National Purpose, intelligently comprehended and acquiesced in—only unselfish Leadership is needed, and, neither control by force nor control by cunning is necessary to bring about the unification of effort needed to accomplish the Nation's Objective.

The significance of this lesson is the utter irrationality of national control in the hands of any class characterized by self-centered instincts, or that strength or skill or cunning should be dominating factors in the social structure.

Though none of these factors should dominate, each and all of these vital and necessary elements should have free scope for the socially effective outflow of its particular expression of life energy.

Second only in significance to the acquiescence and co-operation of the united people is the method irresistibly forced upon the Nation by the logic and necessities of its stupendous War problem.

First Real Nation.

This most modern economic institution, and the unified co-operation of the united people, are the two outstanding lessons of the War for us.

Taken together, they point significantly to the solution of our social problem—the lacking element which should and could consciously, deliberately, and rationally unify the basic instinctive urges into an harmonious direction of national effort and so produce a humanly efficient national organization—the first real Nation on earth!

The lacking element?—the element which is adapted to assume the function and position to be vacated by the obsolescent autocratic concept—arbitrary "control"—the element capable of controlling without control, of making Freedom effective, Democracy a living fact as well as a noble Ideal!

In this, as in many other seem-

ingly difficult problems of long standing, the solution has evaded us by reason of its very obviousness. Such a unifying factor has always existed in plain view—unutilized in its proper function of Social Strain Equalizer. ,Indeed, this urge factor, more even than the Instincts—"to Live," "to Make," "to Take," "to Control"—is the most universal and most humanly characterizing trait of that most marvelous complex—Man.

Desire to Know.

I refer to Curiosity—curiosity rationalized into Desire to Know.

Desire to Know, while equally urgent for gratification, inherently lacks the undesirable and inappropriate qualities which render the other human Instincts unsuitable as organizing and strain equalizing factors in the social structure. Also it possesses qualities and attributes which make it peculiarly adapted to perform the rationally harmonizing function so irrationally assumed in all earlier social organizations under the guise of Forceful and Cunning Control.

Desire to Know is as imperative in its demands as any of the self-centered motor Instincts—to live, to make, to take, to control—but it is impersonal; while it is as aggressive as other Instinctive Urges, characteristically its energies and activities are directed at Nature, not in aggression on human opponents; hence it engenders no human strife; and while it drives furiously, it drives none but its possessor—in the pursuit of Knowledge.

Desire to Know, while profoundly interested in all that pertains to Human Life and living—to eugenics and racial development—characteristically its possessor would risk his own life in the pursuit of Knowledge.

Desire to Know, though urgently interested in Nature's Laws and in all that concerns the correct making and constructing of things, characteristically lacks desire to make or construct things, but seeks only systematized concepts of Knowledge.

Desire to Know, while deeply interested in all that pertains to the desirable things of the world and to economic affairs, characteristically lacks the thievish impulse—the Instinct to Take, to acquire physical possession: supremely acquisitive it craves only to acquire Knowledge.

Desire to Know, while surpassingly Masterful, desires no mastery of Men; it craves instead, God-like insight, pre-vision, prophecy—power in the boundless realms of Knowledge.

Leadership.

Here then is an indomitable Urge lacking all the inappropriate qualities of the strife producing Autocratic Force-and-Fear Control motor concept of Social Organization, and possessed of all the unifying qualities of Social Leadership.

A Human Society or Nation is sanely designed and rationally organized on correct principles only when it has a Purpose, and (as in the case of a well considered machine) only when full cognizance is taken of all its contributory elements, together with their essential functions and their proper co-ordination.

A National Objective.

A truly efficient National Organization would facilitate (not suppress or prohibit) the expression of all inherent Instinctive Urges, rationalizing their outflowing life energy (by sane institutional conventions) into unification in a fully predetermined National Purpose.

In a crude but clearly perceptible manner the United States, during the War, gave suggestion of such an Ideal Social Arrangement.

It had a defined and universally accepted purpose:

Its Scientific (Desire to Know) Men and its Scientific Societies were (more or less) organized into a Unifying and Advisory Board to formulate and suggest methods and means for sane living and—to accomplish the predetermined purpose of the Nation.

We have accomplished the object of the War:

We have made the World safe for Democracy.

Now, let us inaugurate a Democracy—a Democracy with an object for its existence—a Democracy with a Purpose.

By the peril to its life, the Nation has been shocked into momentary sanity. Let us while still rational, rationally take to heart the lessons which the War has taught at so staggering a cost:

First: The need of a National Purpose; a purpose based upon peace and rational Human Development; a purpose as inspiring and as unifying as War for Democracy, and as high as our highest Ideals of Life.

Second: The need of a Supreme National Council of Scientists—supreme over all other National Institutions—to advise and instruct us how best to Live, and how most efficiently to realize our Individual and our National Purpose and Ideals.

But, First and Last, a unifying National Objective.

Fernwald, Berkeley, December, 1918.

IS WEALTH MORE PRECIOUS THAN HUMAN PERSONALITY?
IS IT RATIONAL TO BASE HUMAN SOCIETY
ON ANIMAL INSTINCTS?

Technocracy

PART II.

National Industrial Management.
Practical Suggestions for National Reconstruction.

By William Henry Smyth

NOTE:—After outlining and characterizing the great economic drifts in the national developments of the past, the author declares that during the period of war the United States has developed the new form in government for which there is no precedent in human experience. He calls this "Technocracy"—the organizing, co-ordinating and directing through industrial management on a nation-wide scale of the scientific knowledge and practical skill of all the people who could contribute to the accomplishment of a great national purpose. Carry this new form of government into the days of peace and we will have industrial democracy—a new commonwealth.—Editor.

Economic Drifts.

The United States is obviously in social flux, in unstable economic equilibrium—in transition. Customs and usages which a few years ago received universal approval and legal sanction are now punished as crimes. Economic expedients which but yesterday were deemed irrational imaginations of utopian visionaries are today accomplished facts. And in every direction immemorial methods and time honored social processes have lost their sacrosanctity.

Like ocean streams enfolding in mass-flow all this whirling confusion of economic cross-currents, legal revolutions, and social agitations, there are to be observed certain super-controlling drifts.

Centralization of Government.
Concentration of Wealth.
Unification of Mechanical Industries.

Force, Wealth, Industry.

These great economic drifts indicate the mass resultant of myriad individual activities expressing that peculiarly human quality which has made man the dominating animal factor on earth—unquenchable desire to control—the Mastery Instinct. And what is more important in the present connection, these super-controlling social drifts also indicate the only directions possible for the social expression of this indomitable human urge:

Direct control of men by force and fear—exemplified in Centralization of Government; indirect control of men by controlling their products—shown in Concentration of Wealth; mutualized control (i. e., utilization) of Nature—expressed in Unification of Mechanistic Industries.

Conflicting Ideals.

In these various forms of social aggregations there are, broadly speaking, but three human types involved:
The type characterized by aggressive physical strength; the type characterized by alert mental cunning; the type characterized by purposive skill.

Of these the last—the purposive skill type—is significantly modern, brought into social prominence by that most stupendous social factor, experimental science, science which is the effective cause and basis of this era of invention—our industrial age.

A triangular conflict of ideals of life and of social purpose has thus been inaugurated; a conflict which accounts for and is expressed in our "social unrest," "conflict of capital and labor," our "social problem" and "reconstruction." The strife for supremacy of social ideal and community purpose thus indicated, is co-extensive with the human race; its most spectacular climax is the World War. And notwithstanding the many confusing forms and many-sided aspects which this world-wide human struggle presents, it is, of course, at bottom the ages old contest of Slavery and Liberty, Bondage and Freedom.

The Golden Age?

Our answer to this old but ever new problem will determine whether our industrial age will progress to a social condition of individual freedom to which nothing in the past is comparable, or whether our time shall be, to future generations, the Golden Age!— the highwater mark of human liberty —the age of a noble but a futile fight for a great ideal—Democracy.

Club Economics.

In simple cave-man times the boss-parent, quite naturally, made and administered suitable primitive economics—with his persuasive club as a very practical emblem of authority. Under this raw-force regime the weaker "fagged" for the stronger; and the doings and havings of the "fags" made life more likeable for the forceful.

As the procreator of his subjects— and superior in strength during most of their lives—the "ownership" of them and theirs by the boss-parent was as "natural" as any other obvious fact; and chattel slavery as necessary as parent ownership is self-evident.

Mystery Economics.

Then, Miracle-Fire-Maker and Animal Breeder came along, and disturbed many of the time honored and well established customs—playing havoc generally with club-economics. By his wonder working magics cunning Miracle-worker put the fear of gods (more potent than physical strength) into the heart of simple old skull-cracker parent-god. So Miracle-worker waxed fat, and in his turn initiated and administered suitable economics—fire worship and mystery-economics, otherwise Theocracy.

With theocracy came the greatest of all social revolutions; the dethroning of brute strength and the crowning of mental alertness—Cunning. This marked an epoch in human history, in man's upward progress as a social animal. Also it marked the beginning of control of men (and their products) through man's instinctive

fear of the unknown—the Rule of the Cunning.

Force-Mystery-Economics.

With varying fortunes force-economics and cunning-economics contended for supremacy till in comparatively modern times autocracy was found an effective compromise. In this most practical arrangement, the (by that time conventionalized) parent-god received his authority from the All-powerful God-of-Magic. So was initiated modernized force-mystery-economics. And the human race has as yet found no more efficient means for the control of organized society than force-mystery-economics; methods, means, and institutions which, but superficially modified since old Miracle worker's day, still function in our twentieth century (autocratic and democratic) customs, usages, conventions, and legalized economic systems.

Working-by-proxy-Economics.

In cave-man economics, the real function of the club or the purpose of Club-er was not to incapacitate Club-ee, but to induce the latter to do and supply the matters and things which otherwise would require greater and more constant expenditure of effort on the part of the economist, than the semi-occasional swing of his skull-cracker.

Old Skull-cracker's motives (though more crudely expressed) were the same as mine are, in the employment of my cook and my gardener, that is economy of effort on my part; otherwise working-by-proxy.

But the club-economic-system was essentially wasteful and inefficient: its operating expenses were outrageously high, notwithstanding the low cost of raw (human) material. Indeed, the system was apt to defeat its own ends, especially in those strenuous days, when zeal commonly outran discretion.

Doers and Suppliers.

Thus mystery-coercion represents an enormous economic advance over raw physical force. Fear of unknown but awesome consequences for failure to do and supply matters and things is fully as effective as the club—and beyond measure less wasteful of Doers and Suppliers.

So it is quite natural and inevitable that crude force methods and processes of economic control should lose favor in competition with mystery economic systems. And long race experience has proved that a judicious combination of club and mystery (otherwise force and cunning) makes for the highest degree of efficiency in a Working-by-Proxy economic system.

Proxy-Beneficiaries.

Such economic systems, however, obviously imply direct or indirect slavery—ownership of the body or control of the mind of the proxy. And for the latter the mystery method is peculiarly adapted and most satisfactory.

For self-evident reasons, control over another's mind is more effective and economical than property ownership of his body, taking into consideration the practical responsibility which the latter entails. So quite naturally, direct ownership of Proxy by the economical Worker-by-proxy gives place to customs, usages, and conventions (economics), facilitating control over the results of Proxy's activities.

Then, too, complex division of labor and specialization render chattel slavery impractical, indeed unworkable, in a society highly organized for productive industry. So an ideal working-by-proxy economic system would permit complete physical liberty to do and to make, while arranging appropriate usages, customs, and laws which automatically transfer ownership of the matters and things done and made, from the doers and makers to the proxy-beneficiaries.

Economic Science?

The difference between modern and primordial economics is not in idea or purpose, but only in added obscurity of method and in greater complexity of detail. Incidentally, also, it has become evident that "economics" is not a "science" in any proper sense, but a variable system of community usages intended to facilitate the predominating social activities. And, hence, to be workable an "economic system" must be in keeping with the activities which characterize the times.

In cave-man times, the boss-parent and his club-men had to make cave-economics. A system initiated by the "fags" would have been obviously unworkable. The priesthood had to initiate and administer theocratic economics. And so on, through the various changes in social organization: Those whose activities characterize the times must initiate and administer its economics.

Economic Experiments.

Raw force has been relegated to the economic backwoods—to the racially infantile tribes of darkest Africa, and to the social usages of our anachronistic "criminal elements," the yegg, the thug, the gun-fighter, the strong-arm gangs of the underworld of modern organized society.

Theocracy, with its crude cunning, its childish terrors and its dazzling promises of future (super-mundane) rewards, has practically vanished as a recognized dominant social factor—a fading shadow of ancient greatness.

Autocracy, that cunning combination of force and fear economics, has just now been dumped into the scrap-heap of out-worn social expedients, at the cost of the most atrocious and bloodiest of all wars, and the flower of the World's Manhood.

Plutocracy, with its autocratic capitalistic economics (while weakened and shaken by the shocks and stresses of the World War) is still a virile contestant for the throne of World Dominion.

Strength, Skill, Cunning.

Economics efficient for autocracy must necessarily differ from economics appropriate to theocracy; and these would differ from economics suitable for plutocracy; and these again would differ still more from economics appropriate to and efficient for Industrial Democracy. In brief: Force-economics, Cunning-economics, and Skill-economics must necessarily differ as widely as the essential differences between the basic qualities, Strength, Cunning, Skill.

Hence any attempt to organize or "re-construct" a social aggregation with these three basic human traits as contemporary economic bases means simply continual social warfare; a war which, sooner or later, must be decided by victory for the Strong, the Cunning, or the Skilled—unless human ingenuity can devise a form of society which will permit and facilitate the full, unified, and socially useful expression of these three irrepressible forms of life energy.

Mechanized Industry.

Thus we return to the three great social drifts:

Centralization of Government;

Concentration of Wealth;

Unification of Mechanistic Industries..

Of the first two little need be said, for they are familiar racial experiences. But the last—the mechanizing of life—is quite otherwise; hence it is, if for no other reason, the most significant factor to be taken into account in the social problems with which we are now confronted—our problem of economic reconstruction.

And, truly, our modern mechanization of human life is a most dubious social experiment—a danger-fraught development—a dynamitic racial adventure.

Modern Science.

Back of the mechanizing of human functioning is that greatest of all modern marvels—experimental science.

Science has brought about a profound revolution in our mental attitude toward life, and in our methods of dealing with nature. It has swept into the discard practically all our previous notions regarding ourselves and our relations to the laws of nature—to Universal Reality. It has, at the same time, debased man's pride in the dust of humility, and glorified intelligence and human worth to God-like heights.

Science is, of course, the effective cause of our present mechanistic development—with all its physical benefits and all its spiritual horrors; for science knows neither morals nor ethics, and is equally potent for social "bad" as for social "good."

Science works just as effectively in criminal hands as in those of a saint. It is an impersonal, ethically neutral force and factor so potent that—even in the chaotic condition in which it now exists—it has brought about a world revolution in man's mental outlook and his physical activities, both individually and collectively. Indeed it has shown to man a new Heaven, a new Earth, and a new Hell.

Our social Heaven we have yet to construct, but the World War is sufficiently impressive proof of what social Hell can be wrought by Science in the hands of self-interest.

Past and Present.

As the result of modern science, the present time is without precedent, hence no valid analogy exists or can be imagined between an economic system appropriate to our science-taught mechanistic age and earlier economic systems suitable to conditions of life, the warp, woof, and pattern of which were Mystery, Magic, Chance.

That no helpful comparison can be made between the past and the present would be completely true, were it not that our science teachings affect but the thinnest superficial layer of our conscious thinking, while the

There is a serenity, a long view on the part of science, which seems to be of no age, but to carry human thought along from generation to generation, freed from the elements of passion. Every just mind must condemn those who so debase the studies of men in science as to use them against humanity and, therefore, it is part of your task and of ours to reclaim science from this disgrace, to show that she is devoted to the advancement and interest in humanity and not to its embarrassment and destruction. The spirit of science is a spirit of seeking after truth so far as the truth is ready to be applied to human circumstances.

From President Wilson's address before the Academy of Lincei in Rome.

fabric of our thought processes, our familiar customs, our current usages, our economic institutions remain practically unchanged—our racial heritage.

But, even so, the unceasing conflict of past and present, of slavery and freedom, of bondage and liberty, of error and truth, goes ever on and on—a blood soaked path; a path of misery, strife and disappointment, though hopefully ever upward toward our ideal—Industrial Democracy with personal freedom for Self-realization.

Mental Inertia.

Without a concurrent change of economic institutions appropriate to the amazingly rapid psychical development and refinement of our modern ideals—brought about by the advent of science—the realization of these ideals will be impossible. And sorrowfully we recognize that man's instinctive resistance to change of old established modes of thought—howsoever irrational—makes progress in this direction seem almost hopeless.

Familiar Fallacies.

Most reluctantly are familiar fallacies relinquished, indeed, we hang on to them with irrational tenacity ages after their unworkable character has time and again been tragically demonstrated.

As in our bodily functions and skeletal frame there still persist the characteristics of our Saurian primordial ancestry, so ancient modes of thought live unnoted in our present day thinking processes; and our social institutions represent the seemingly outgrown superstitions constituting man's mental heredity during every past age since the infancy of the human race.

"Gott mit uns."

Medievalism characterizes our sacred and secular institutions and energizes our customary · actions. Demonology is practically as prevalent as in the past; unnoted in ourselves but easily perceived in the "Gott mit uns" attitude of the Kaiser.

We pray for health, heedless of nature's laws; we pray for long life while disregarding the simple rules of right living; we beseech forgiveness of "sin" while making sin profitable by deliberate legal enactment. In a world filled to overflowing with all good and humanly desirable things to be had for the striving, we economically steal from our industrious neighbors; like paupers we beg "God" for vicariously earned joys, for uncarned prosperity, and for all other forms of undeserved "good fortune;" and like pert children we urge silly advice on our man-made Providence, for the conduct of common human affairs, which we are too lazy, too stupid, too self-indulgent to bring to desired outcome by our own effort.

The God of Chance.

Important departments of life and the distribution of the products of industry—trade, speculation, opportunity, recreation—involve large elements of "luck," for by grotesquely solemn "laws" the issues are left to the "God of Chance." Just precisely as in the old days when momentous matters were settled by the entrails of sacrificial animals.

The killing of President McKinley by a madman "caused" the depreciation in the value of stocks to the extent of thousands of millions of dollars; the San Francisco calamity —which rendered half a million human beings homeless—"made" fortunes for the owners of and speculators in suburban property; the Titanic disaster threw a hundred millions of wealth (others' products) into the hands of a school-boy, and with it control over the lives of thousands of human beings; and even the supreme tragedy of a World at War is the prolific "cause" of transforming hundreds of mediocre men into multi-millionaires—and hence into powerful social factors.

Diabolism.

All this represents kindergarten thinking, primitive and childish as nursery prattle of prixies and fairies, Aladin's lamp, and all the other forms of Old World superstition and diabolism, worthy only of the infancy of the race.

Were it not that these grotesqueries characterize our "economic and finance system" and our solemn Professors soberly teach them, they would be utterly incredible in this Age of Science and Mechanics.

But, as already indicated, our "economics and finance" are merely survivals from pre-science times; an inheritance from the days of wizardry and witchcraft, mystery and magic.

Our quaint "economics" and queer "finance" are as anachronistic, as inconsistent, and as ineffective in this Mechanical Age of Industrialism, as astrology would be in an astronomical observatory, alchemy in a chemical laboratory or "perpetual motion" in a machine shop.

Scientific Foresight.

Imagination based on science enables us to foresee the oak in the acorn—coming events latent in present happenings. But so strong is custom, so firm is the grip of the past, so compelling is the obsession of ancient superstitions, that—with all our lately acquired capability for rational scientific thinking—only the tragedy of the accomplished fact has sufficient power to jolt our sluggard wits into momentary activity.

Ten, fifteen, yes, twenty-five years ago, it required no more intelligence to foresee the present war than to anticipate a crop in the Fall from seed sown in the Spring.

Even less scientific imagination is now needed to foretell a condition of social disintegration, one more widespread and disastrous than the War, as the logical and inevitable outcome of our irrational and antiquated social conventions—our "economic and financial system."

Taking Instinct.

If taking—by force or diverting by cunning, in whole or in part—the product of another's effort, without adequate equitable return, be accepted as a valid social principle of action between individuals, it must be equally good and proper as between social groups, as between nations.

But however disguised in smooth sounding phrases—the "chances of business," the "profits of trade," the "opportunity of others' misfortune," the "prize of the victor," the "fortunes of war," the "right of might"—taking expresses the parasitic and predatory instincts. And, called by whatsoever name or howsoever disguised, taking others' makings by force, or diverting others' products by stealthy cunning, inevitably involves unending strife; strife within the group and recurring wars of nations—strife to settle the relative strength or cunning as between individuals, and wars to determine the relative might of nations.

Predatory Economics.

Our "economic system" is essentially autocratic in means, in method, in objective. Being a left-over from an Age of Predatory Autocracy, necessarily its ideals are materialistic—its motor instinct and urge impulse being self-centered "greed and grab." Naturally its means are force and cunning and its methods are ruthless, for its object is power—power, irresponsible and absolute.

Our Modern Ideals.

If we are to remain true to our ideals—ideals which the flame of war has illumined to our normally purblind spiritual insight—our course is determined. We have no choice but to choose freedom: pioneer a virgin trail, slash a course unblazed by history, uncharted in race experience—a courage testing National Adventure.

The race has never before been confronted with a situation in any way analogous to the one in which we now find ourselves, nor a problem the like of that which we are now compelled to solve; yes, and solve correctly, if we would avoid distintegration into social chaos—overwhelmed by a science-made Frankenstein.

Science Is Dynamitic!

Science has, however, put into our hands an instrumentality of such immeasurable potency, that, used with intelligent courage, we may conquer all our difficulties, surmount all our social obstructions.

But, Science left to chance, or in the hands of unintelligent self-interest, the chances are it will work untold social calamity.

There are so many roads to go wrong, and only one way to go right.

To leave a force and factor of such supreme social significance and potentiality as Science in its present condition—socially uncontrolled and unorganized for the commonweal— is more crassly unintelligent than to permit fused and capped dynamite to be scattered around promiscuously, to the chances of any carelessly or maliciously applied spark.

(A striking and significant parallelism to the thought here expressed was subsequently voiced by President Wilson in one of his speeches at the Versailles Peace Conference:

"Is it not a startling circumstance, for one thing, that the quiet studies of men in laboratories, that the thoughtful developments which have taken place in quiet lecture rooms, have now been turned to the destruction of civilization?

"The enemy whom we have just overcome had at his seats of learning some of the principal centers of scientific study and discovery, and he used them in order to make destruction sudden and complete; and only the watchful, continuous co-operation of men can see to it that science as well as armed men are kept within the harness of civilization.")

Democracy.

In the rough, Democracy is the rule of the mob, the rule of the masses, the rule of the majority—the rule of un-intelligence. But even so, it is better than any form of governmental control based upon self-interest—not excepting "Beneficent Autocracy."

Humanly bad and socially inefficient as it may be, and has been, Democracy alone encloses and fosters the living germ of freedom—self- government.

But, during the scant two years that we were at war, no ordinary or accepted definition of Democracy could make that term descriptive of the United States; indeed, under the life threatening stress of a World War, our great but chaotic nation—in self-preservation—ceased to be a Democracy!

Transformation.

In that remarkable war transformation, we certainly did not become an Autocracy; even less so a Plutocracy; and least of all a Theocracy. In fact, during this thrillingly interesting time, the United States developed into a form of "Government" for which there is no precedent in human experience.

National Industrial Management —Technocracy.

The characterizing peculiarity which rendered our great country unique— during this period of national stress— and not only unique but uniquely irresistible, was the fact that we rationally organized our National Industrial Management. We became, for the time being, a real Industrial Nation.

This we did by organizing and co-ordinating the Scientific Knowledge, the Technical Talent, the Practical Skill and the Man Power of the entire Community: focusing them in the National Government, and applying this Unified National Force to the accomplishment of a Unified National Purpose.

For this unique experiment in rationalized Industrial Democracy I have coined the term "Technocracy."

It was but an experiment—a forced one—to meet an exceptionally serious emergency; and like most other experimental devices, it doubtless was far from perfect in many ways and details. Still, as it seems to me, it presented an important suggestion, the germ of a novel and significant idea— a pioneer idea in the ancient art of government.

Dog-Eat-Dog.

Until appropriate economic institutions and instrumentalities are available, humanly effective Industrial Democracy must remain an unrealizable ideal, a theory unattainable as a work-a-day principle of social life, and for the efficient distribution of the products of toil, upon which human life rests.

The practical working out of our present efforts in this direction, has so far only resulted in a frenzied scramble for wealth, place, power—a brutish-instinct-scramble, in which greed, cunning, and lust for human mastery are the urges; "dog-eat-dog" the "practical" ideal; and mystery, m e d i e v a l i s m, law-loaded-dice and chuck-a-luck instrumentalities the controlling factors.

The Greedless Scientist.

In this weird social (?) conglomeration how incongruous seems—and, indeed, is—the greedless scientist, who seeks but to learn, to comprehend, and to co-ordinate the laws of nature; and who cares naught for human mastery. In this frenzied scramble for science-created wealth what earthly chance has its real creator—the scientist?

Practically none!

None, unless he sells himself into virtual slavery; unless he debauches his truth-seeking to the interest of those who—more "practical"—devote their energy and cunning to the "practical" enterprise of gaining power by securing control of wealth. And yet, the United States is characteristically a nation of technologists—scientists, inventors, workers in and utilizers of the raw materials and the forces of nature. Not only are we instinctively mechanistic, but we are—by heritage, by force of circumstance, and by tradition—born lovers of personal freedom. Freedom is our ideal—self-government.

Prior to the War, our de-humanizing ideal was Mechanistic Efficiency, under its soul-searching stress was born a Humanly Effective Nation.

Our Costly Lesson.

With all these considerations before us, and our fleeting glance at the possibilities of socially unified skill, technology, and science, how worse than foolish to revert to our pre-War "dog-eat-dog" practices and practical (?) ideals.

Instead of so doing, would it not be well to take to heart the lessons forced upon us at so stupendous a cost of life and human misery?

Would it not be wise statesmanship to experiment further on the lines of direction into which we were forced by the compulsions and stresses of War?

Reconstruction—With a National Objective.

The War is over—won!

We are now facing the—in reality—more stupendous problems of social reconstruction.

For the War, we enlisted, conscripted, commandeered all our men who by natural aptitude, and by personal inclination, were adapted to the requirements of war. We organized and co-ordinated them for the intended purpose; we trained and exercised their bodies and their minds to meet known and unknown trials; we energized their loyalty to the Flag—the Commonweal; we stirred their personal devotion to the Nation's ideals; we enthused their wills to the accomplishment of the unified Will of the Nation —the National Objective.

Rationalized Industrial Democracy.

No need is there to speak of the result of this Unification of National Spirit and National Purpose—the War is over; won!—gloriously won!

As we enlisted all those peculiarly adapted to the destructive functions of War, let us now systematically unify those peculiarly adapted to the constructive functions of Peace—our scientists, our technologists, our inventors, indeed, all who by natural aptitude and personal inclination are specially fitted to deal with the social and constructive problems of peaceful industry; nationally unify them and their accomplishments for the Commonweal.

Let us organize our scientists, our technologists, our exceptionally skilled; let us commandeer, conscript, enlist, their loyalty, their devotion, their enthusiasm, their intelligence, their interest, their talents, their accomplishments for the purposes of Peace and the realization of a Noble National Purpose.

Let us rationalize our Industrial Democracy!

Public Service First.

We are up against the problem of national reconstruction; let us not tinker with futile details—let us nationally Re-construct.

Such a national co-ordination of Science and Technology, as is here suggested, would produce and constitute a living and Social life-giving National Reservoir of Science—practical and theoretical; a Technical Army devoted to Peace and Construction.

It would constitute a National Army, from which alone Private Interests could draw their needed scientific and technical personnel; personnel whose loyalty is primarily to the Commonweal—the Nation; the Nation of which they are honored Public Servants.

This is the exact reverse of our present unpatriotic, un-democratic order and organization. Yet, such an intimate, but subsidiary, relation to public service, as is suggested, would liberate not hamper individual energy and freedom of private enterprise, for it would permit the free expression of self-interest unified in the commonweal. Also it would, without conflict, facilitate the full and socially useful outflow of the three vigorous forms of life energy—Strength, Skill, Cunning.

Industrial Apex.

From this co-ordinated Army of Science, Technology, and Skill should be selected (by a process of realized capability and recognized social worth) a representative and comprehensive National Council of Scientists as Managing Directors—our Supreme Social Institution.

Fernwald, Berkeley, January, 1919.

This National Council should be the apex of the Nation's Industrial Management. It should constitute the Leadership of our thus rationalized Industrial Democracy.

Purpose.

But this reconstruction — revolutionary as it doubtless will appear to many—is only preparation for our National Task.

It would, indeed, make of us an organized human aggregation—a unified social machine, capable of intelligent self-conscious national life; and then comes the question:

For what worthy purpose have we constructed this huge highly organized Human Instrumentality?

This problem a Nation—no less than an individual—unescapably faces, the instant it has become really self-determining.

It is the Nation's first, its final, its only problem—the final problem of human existence.

And this all-important matter, every Nation (like every individual) must settle for itself—settle between itself and Universal Rationality: The object of the Nation's being; its conscious rational purpose—its National Objective.

SHOULD THE DESTINY OF THE NATION
BE LEFT TO CHANCE?

Technocracy

PART III.

Ways and Means
To Gain Industrial Democracy.

By William Henry Smyth

NOTE:—In the two preceding essays Mr. Smyth forecasts a new form of government that he calls "Technocracy"—National Industrial Management. This article discusses ways and means to develop, guide and direct purposive industrial democracy and so usher in a new commonwealth.

The author suggests three practical thoughts for economic reconstruction: That permitting chance to influence our lives and conditions means ignorance. That the flow of time is not reversible—the future cannot help the present. That cause and effect, not whim, is the law in nature's processes.—Editor.

Social Structures.

Democracy and Autocracy are the antitheses of social organization and express opposite underlying principles of human interaction.

The structural details of any human contrivance—whether Mechanical or Sociological—must be in keeping with its underlying idea. Change in principle necessarily entails functional re-organization—reconstruction.

Hence, ways and means that have proved effective for autocracy, or that long usage has shaped to facilitate its aims and outcomes, must needs be not only unworkable in, but subversive of, democracy. So it will be helpful in our quest to keep constantly and clearly in mind the differences between these mutually exclusive notions of Government.

Autocracy.

Probably the most radical difference between these two forms of social structures is the assumed sources from which each gets its authority.

Autocracy derives its powers from "God." This assumption pre-supposes inherent social distinctions between individuals — occult privileges conferred upon some to control the acts of others. But effectively to control acts makes requisite control of thoughts, for consecutive thought necessarily precedes purposive action.

Thus Autocracy implies a "God-given" right of censorship over other men's physical and mental functioning. Hence, it also pre-supposes the non-neutrality of Nature — cosmic-favoritism; for clearly nature's "God" could not look with favor upon disobedience or lack of submission to the mandates of His authorized agents.

A social organization framed upon this general idea implies constructive details, i. e., customs, laws, institutions —economics—comprising:

1. A Supreme Control element, deriving its authority from and responsible only to a super-mundane source.

2. Social instrumentalities to enforce obedience—physically coerce human actions, and super-naturally control men's thoughts.

3. A descending series of conferred authority starting with the "God-appointed Ruler" and ending with the popular "masses" void of rights.

Thus the measure of efficiency in this social system is the absoluteness of control — completeness of enforced obedience in act and subservience in thought to the "God-inspired will" of the Autocrat and his Agents.

Democracy.

Democracy derives its authority from Man. This pre-supposes general intelligence sufficient at least for self-conscious Individual wants and Mass purposes, with freedom for their pursuit; thus it assumes super-mundane non-interference with human wants and purposes, and a rational Cosmic Order corresponding or co-ordinated to human intelligence in suchwise as to be knowable and responsive thereto.

A social system based upon this general idea implies constructive details in consonance with:

1. The neutrality of nature.
2. Inherent individual rights flowing from the facts of rational human existence.
3. Equality of individual rights.

Thus the measure of efficiency in a Democracy is to be gaged by the completeness of individual freedom of thought and liberty of action in relation to each other and of access to nature's stores, resources and forces—freedom and liberty being based upon rationality as determined by workability in the production of general human happiness, prosperity and opportunity for self-development.

Autocracy is based upon the idea of the essential manship (i. e. manlikeness) of "God" and the inherent unrighteousness—irrationality—of Man.

Democracy is based upon the idea of the essential God-ship (i. e. Godlikeness) of Man and the inherent righteousness—rationality—of the Universe.

Thus we get a clear concept of our chosen social Ideal, and from it indications as to the character of means appropriate to or discordant therewith. In other words we have on broad lines, bases for rational economic conventions, adapted to make effective a social system on the basic principles of Democracy.

Limitations.

Neither by mutual agreement, nor by legal enactment, nor by constitutional provision, nor even as a concession to ancient custom and universal consent may we make two units and two units constitute five units—being contrary to the facts of nature. For precisely the same reasons we cannot (by any or all of these social expedients) successfully adopt or retain economic devices at variance with the essential principles of Democracy.

Industrial Democracy—Purpose.

Autocracy and Democracy are both merely forms of human organization, group contrivances—social machines—built on different basic ideas or principles; machines to accomplish something.

A Nation (no less than an individual) that would build (or "reconstruct") without first clearly determining the purpose of the proposed structure, would be indulging in a foolish and futile waste of energy. But what our national purpose is, is quite apart from the present inquiry. And, indeed, it is not the province of an individual, but of consensus to determine the ultimate National Objective.

Industrial Democracy.

The people of the United States have, however, agreed and decided upon the idea of the National Organization and its proximate character — Industrial Democracy. Or perhaps this outcome represents the resultant of choice and circumstance. Be that as it may, we are now consciously launched on a career of mechanistic Industrial Democracy; and the aim of the present inquiry is to investigate the functional consistency (appropriateness) of the working parts to the accepted principle of the National Social Machine.

Neutral Nature.

The greatest and most consequence-breeding thought that has ever found lodgement in the human mind is the idea that: Nature is neutral toward Man and in regard to all Human concerns.

The greatest and most consequential human discovery is: The Orderliness—rationality—of Nature.

These two concepts are the marvelously fruitful germs from which all modern Science has developed. And, as exact science—based upon experimental proof—owes its continued development to machines of precision; it may with ultimate significance be said that our idea and Ideal of Human Liberty, self-government, as we today conceive it, is one of the many wonderful products of the machine shop—our Mechanistic Industrialism.

Motor Impulse of Autocracy.

Man's soul is free, hence Rational Liberty is his social motor impulse.

Clearly, with an anthropomorphic "God" interested in human wants, wishes, purposes, and projects, and with unlimited power and inclination to meddle in human concerns, to help or hinder, to make or mar them; human "freedom of thought" would be futile, and human "liberty of action" a farce.

We have seen that the motor impulse of Autocracy is super-mundane in origin; its initiative is superhuman; its means are mysterious occult powers derived from "above"; that privilege maintained by ruthless force and cunning is an essential element; and power absolute and humanly irresponsible is its objective.

These factors therefore present some criteria wherewith to gauge the validity of present economic conventions; also to test their appropriateness in a Democracy, the basis of which is human experience energized by individual human initiative; likewise to measure their probable worth in a society in which the powers to do, and the opportunity to be, are derived from the consensus of free and equal human wills; wills subject to none, but co-operating to facilitate individual and mutual purposes—purposes socially unified in the purposive National Will.

Nature Non-Ethical.

In the light of Modern Science, human experience shows that Nature's dealings with Man carry no more moral or ethical significance than in the problems of Practical Mechanics. Scientifically enlightened experience teaches that Humanity alone is ethical or takes account of motives:

Impartially the sun warms and scorches, blesses or blasts; brings famine and plenty, life and death. The sea, the wind, earthquake and torrent, and all the forces of Nature build and destroy, with utter disregard to Man or his handiworks, his hopes or his faiths, his motives or his morals. The wondrous mechanism of Creative Evolution performs its myriad functions no less oblivious to Man's existence than are the ponderous machines of Man's own devising. Nature, like them, fosters or overwhelms with heedless indifference; ruthless, pitiless, appalling to ignorance, error, and fear; but helpful, indulgent, obedient to knowledge, intelligence and courage; neither kind nor cruel, nor good, nor bad—impersonal.

Failure.

In the past, with childlike faith we have relied for support and guidance in human affairs upon the assumed beneficence of occult Powers. Upon this basis, Autocracy is the only conceivable form of social organization.

Yet, the autocratic idea and Ideal has proven, (in the opinion of many), to be a disastrous failure under modern conditions; and we in the United States have decided to try its antithesis—Democracy.

But while discarding the old for the new Ideal, we have, most illogically, retained—substantially unchanged—the effective conventions, the ways and means, of the old order.

And now, with modern Science and Mechanics—hindered and hampered at all points by our futile and inappropriate "Economic System"—we are fighting for National life and Democracy against efficiently organized Autocracy. Not alone the Autocracy of organized military force but also the Autocracy of systematized and unified financial Cunning.

Thus the urgent need for scientific reconstruction of our whole social system is multiplied manyfold, if we are to rectify our past sins against reason and retrieve our pitiful social failure.

Modern Dependence on Machinery.

The life of the ordinary modern man differs from that of all previous times in his peculiar dependence upon complicated machinery — machinery over which he exercises no personal control. The manifold activities which in past times depended upon individual muscular effort are now performed by prime movers and power driven machines, so that the individual man's work and effort is unmeaning and useless apart from these instrumentalities of life and production.

Thus the United States is one huge mechanistic industrial workshop..

The organization of these complex, specialized, power-driven mechanisms and the sources of power and of the raw materials with and upon which they operate, together with the distribution of the output, are the functions of Scientific and Technical Industrial Management.

There should be, it would seem, no room or occasion in such an arrangement, for chance, mystery or magic.

Old Customs.

That the average individual prefers old customs to new, helps to account for much that is strange in present conditions; but it fails to explain completely how it happens that occultism has been wholly banished from the Machine Shop—the Social Producing Element—and remains so conspicuously interwoven in our "Economics"—the Social Distributive Element.

It would seem that we are compelled to assume that our deep seated human instinct of self-interest is the controlling factor in maintaining this incongruous combination of Science and Occultism.

It would seem that the cunning acquisitive instinct of certain exceptionally alert minded men in the community—taking advantage of the normal preference of the average man for old ways and customs, and his preoccupation in his favorite workings and doings—is employing these ancient and familiar usages to befog and obscure the stealthy diversion of an undue proportion of the Community Product.

If this be so, it should be interesting to glance at the ways and means, the prestidigitatorial bag-o-tricks by which it is accomplished. Later we will scrutinize them more closely and in greater detail.

Money and Credit.

The bases of Mechanics in all its simple and complex expressions are two commonplace elements — the Wedge and the Lever; the bases of our Economic and Financial System in all its curious manifestations are also two commonplace elements—"Money" and "Credit."

Here the similarity ends.

There is not on ordinary fourteen-year-old school boy in the United States but who knows and intelligently uses the wedge and lever; and there does not exist a Mechanical Expert who could reasonably question the practical accuracy of the boy's knowledge regarding these elements of mechanics.

Under our present economic usages, customs and laws, each one of us—man, woman and child—is compelled, willy-nilly, to use daily and hourly some form of "money" and "credit"; and there is not in the world a man who understands either of these economic elements, as the boy knows the wedge and lever. Nor is there an Economic Specialist or Financial Expert whose attempted explanation of either "money" or "credit" (or the functions of either) whose supposed elucidation would not be ridiculed and controverted by a multitude of Economic and Monetary Experts of equal or greater authority.

The average man of affairs—Lawyer, Doctor, Editor, Tradesman, Merchant or Mechanic—freely admits his incapacity to understand the "mysteries of finance," and frankly says: "I don't know a damn thing about it." Even Bankers and Brokers, Financiers and Economists, whose business it is to deal in and manipulate these most remarkable commodities, will quite frequently make the same honest confession of ignorance. Indeed, the subject is common stock in the jokesmith's workshop.

Mystery, Magic—Failure.

In no other department of human interest is so much mystery, confusion and controversy regarding the basic "facts" and assumptions, except possibly institutional religion—which, avowedly, rests upon the miraculous and supernatural. Indeed, the parallelism between these two ancient activities is curiously complete. Both transcend human experience, and neither submits to the tests of Science—weighing, measuring, cause-and-effect experimental proof.

"Credit."

Like our religious forms, our Economic System is hoary with age—a survival from ancient Babylonian customs. It rests on assumptions unsanctioned by science; its effects are causeless; the miraculous supersedes natural causation; mystery takes the place of human reason; and endless futurity is its heavenly storehouse of all humanly desirable things.

A Thievish Process.

From this miraculous store the "Wizard of Finance," with his wonder-working wand—"Credit"—filches back (for a slight present tangible consideration and without the owners' consent) the imagined products of imagined future toil of unborn generations of workers—a doubly thievish process, as black in morals as in magic.

"Money"

While supposedly representing lifeless things (that wear out by use), "money" is conventionally endowed (by financial magic) with everlasting life, and also with life's unique function — reproduction. So "M o n e y makes money" for ever and ever—for the Magician.

Peace, super-abundance, and endless idleness—"retirement from business"—is "the Promised Land, flowing with milk and honey" of Economic Sainthood—the earthly Heaven of "Finance."

But . . ! Never was work more urgent nor idleness less common; never was peace more scarce nor strife so universal; the labor of future generations has been crazily "mortgaged" by thievish "economic" (!) conventions beyond all possibility of redemption (in spite of the fact that science and mechanics have multiplied manifold the effectiveness and productiveness of present labor); and Man's present vocation is social suicide—the destruction of wealth and the slaughter of his fellow men!

A stupendous and tragic record of "Economic" folly and failure!.

The Mechanic's Philosophy—Success.

The "God" of our nursery tradition has been banished from the Machine Shop and the world of Mechanics. The result of this courageous spiritual Declaration of Independence has been our "Conquest of Nature," our Age of Productive Industry.

Seemingly a like rending of thought shackles, a similar breaking of mental prison bars, is needed in the realm of Economics.

When scientific imagination and knowledge of Nature's Laws are substituted in our economics for chance, mystery, and magic; when the regulation of our Nation-wide industry is taken out of the hands of quibbling "lawyers", and nature's forces, resources, and the mechanical instrumentalities for their transformation into human necessaries and desirables are no longer the play-things of money-juggling gamblers, and the products of Nature and Mechanic Arts no longer glut the instinctive craving of Acquisitive Cunning; when this economic childish irrationality is sanely substituted by organized Science, Technology, and specialized Skill co-ordinated in National Industrial Management, then will begin real civilization, the Age of Social Sanity, —Technocracy.

"Chance" Catastrophes.

The "God of Chance" or "God's mysterious providence"—which permits the killing of a President by a madman; the obliteration of a great city by fire; the sinking of a huge passenger-ship in mid-ocean; and a world-war—are merely misleading euphemisms for human ignorance, human improvidence, and childish shirking of responsibility.

Social conventions—our Economic and Financial system—which by "money magic" make these "chance" catastrophes into controlling factors in the distribution of the product of human effort, are simply tragic monuments to ignorant superstition, mental laziness, and criminal folly.

Indeed, our whole "Economic System" is so incredibly unscientific, so irrational, so utterly puerile, that, were it not for custom-induced mental myopia, its glaring absurdities would long ago have sufficed—without a world-war—to shock our moral sense and intelligence into effectivity.

"Chance" in Economics.

A machine is certain in action and

uniform in output, because scientific imagination has foreseen, and constructive intelligence has provided for, the elimination of the "chance" element.

The forces which will devastate the results of man's industry, through the "natural" action of an uncontrolled torrential stream, (with equal unconcern) if scientifically directed, will make the same country-side teem with human happiness—but, not by "chance." In like manner, the same "natural" social forces which make poverty, wretchedness, and vice, will (with equal unconcern) produce the opposite results—but never by "chance."

Human institutions founded upon "chance" merely express Man's brute-unintelligence. That our "Economic System" makes "chance" a controlling factor for the distribution of wealth, merely shows the persistence of ignorance and that old habits of thought are more compelling than modern intelligence. To legalize "chance" deliberately is to relinquish our Godlike control over the results of Nature's processes, and thus voluntarily enslave ourselves to ruthless Nature, and to abandon even our authority over the outcomes of our own actions. Hence, it would seem, that the first step toward a new and Rational Economics is a courageous declaration of our freedom from tyranny of the insensate "God of Chance."

Choice.

When a Mechanic has decided upon an idea or principle as the basis of a proposed machine, he has exercised his rational freedom of choice. Regardless of whether his choice is wise or not (in this decision) he has placed definite limits upon the range of subsequent selection in regard to detail instrumentalities. Indeed, he has entered into an implied contract—assumed a rational responsibility—to employ only such means in the construction of his machine as (in accord with Universal Order) are appropriate to make effective his proposed mechanical contrivance; with failure as the penalty for wilful or ignorant error—breach of his implied contract.

History demonstrates conclusively that races, nations, civilizations (equally with individuals), are subject to the same rational limitations, are bound by the same responsibility, and incur the same penalty for wilful or ignorant error in exercising their human freedom of choice.

Out Last Warning!

The practical difficulties of forestalling the hazards of birth, of death, and of disaster, are doubtless great, and the problem of eliminating the "chance" element from our economic system is a man-sized job—with a slim probability of complete success. But, it is reasonably certain, that, if courage to make the needed change is lacking, or if our intelligence is insufficient for the task, our social adventure in Democracy will prove a tragedy. And the world war is, I believe, our last warning.

Laisser Faire.

Nor may we drift; laisser faire is lazy fear—cowardly re-submission to the dog-eat-dog jungle law, right-of might principle of Nature—and of Autocracy—from which our modern conscience has revolted.

The Mechanic.

While caution bids us pause and realize that Nature is ruthless in its punishment of ignorance and error, courage reminds us that Nature also is infinitely lavish in its rewards for knowledge and intelligence; and courage points to the Practical Mechanic as an exemplar and an object-lesson for the Social Constructor.

Mechanic vs. Nature

The Mechanic has courageously invaded Nature's guarded realm; has accepted her "no quarter" terms; and has assumed complete responsibility for his revolt against all the ancient Occult Powers.

He has tacitly assumed that "God" and "Nature" are supremely and pre-eminently self-sufficing; that these all-inclusive profundities utterly transcend the utmost limits of his acts or his art—that the "plans of God" and the Mechanic's problems cannot in anywise conflict.

He predicates that "God" and "Nature" are limitlessly competent to care for their own infinite concerns; hence, that his problems, involve only what the Mechanic wants, and not "the wants of God." In so far as concerns his art (and with reverence for Universal Order, which makes his art possible) the Mechanic, in effect, says: "This I will," "Thus I do," "I am the Earth-god of things, of matter, and of motion."

The Mechanic's Achievements

And how gloriously has the Mechanic made good!

Even the most most cursory survey of his accomplishments, in manufacture, in transportation, in communication, in reclamation, in power utilization generally, staggers while it exalts the mind.

Has he not with wheat and corn from Eastern steppe and Western prairie, and with fresh and wholesome meat from the Antipodes, fed the hungry workers of Europe; and brought from the four corners of the Earth materials for their needs, their uses, and their industries? Yes! And from the teeming estuaries of the North he has served the World's table with dainty fish, and with wine and oil and luscious fruit from the fertile valleys of the Pacific Slope.

By his use of Nature's forces, he has immeasurably out-rivalled imagination's Magic Carpet, transporting by his mechanisms untold millions of work-weary families from cramped and life-worn areas to the free spaciousness of many wide scattered Edens of plenty, there to found Empires.

And more, he has bound these broadcast settlements in bonds of mutual help with space-negating bands of steel and steam; and on the one-time pathless ocean he has marked out highways with light and life of swift-moving commerce, till, in the uttermost ends of the earth, friend greets friend as though but a mile from home. Seas no longer separate, nor continents divide, for Man now talks with Man as face to face across the soundless void.

As with a broom, he has swept sullen ocean back to its deeps and bared Netherland's fertile plains; and with dyke, and mill, and pump he holds his prize secure from angry wave and wind and shifting sand. A prize indeed!—a rich and prosperous country of towns and villages, of farms and homesteads, all interlaced with road and rail and placid water-way; a hive of human industry — a kingdom snatched from ocean's grasp.

In torrid Egypt, too, he has tamed the turgid Nile to flood the desert sands and made thereof a nation's granary.

He has moved mountains, split continents, harnessed Niagaras to his machines; subdued the land, triumphed over the sea, and now seeks dominion of the air.

And, East and West and North and South he has sluiced and swept with giant streams the high-piled gravels, and ript and smashed and ground to powder, fine as from the mills of the gods, mountains of crystalline quartz; and dredged, and plowed, and sifted the frozen Arctic tundra, to tear from reluctant Earth its golden treasure for counters wherewith to play Man's world-wide commerce game.

The Economist's Failure.

All this stupendous output of human experience, human reason, human industry—rivalling creation itself —is in startling contrast with our world-wide tragedy, the outcome of our world-wide economics. A contrast doubly significant; significant in the entire absence of chance, of mystery, of magic from the work of the mechanic; and again as expressing the practical extremes of glorious success and of failure most tragic.

Selective Rejection.

The human mind, like the body, can advance only step by step, from the solid ground of the known and tested to the doubtful footing of the unfamiliar. Human progress is like adventuring through a morass of ignorance toward a far-distant goal; with disaster the penalty for every false step.

In the great adventure called "Human Progress" the "Occult" has proved a will-o-the-wisp guide.

Notwithstanding all the stupendous accomplishments which characterize productive industry and the present era as the Age of Mechanics, the process which has brought it all about, is the same step-by-step—

proof by experiment — scientific method. We can think of the new and unknown only in terms of the old and familiar.

Still errors detected and fallacies perceived are guides for inventive synthesis—construction.

Selection is but a process of inverted rejection. So having determined that our ideal social structure is the antithesis of the Autocratic idea, we may with confidence assume that the characteristic elements of Autocracy are inappropriate for our purpose. Thus by a process of (selective) rejection we should arrive at economic expedients more in harmony with our Social Ideal.

Democracy vs. Anarchy.

Universal Order is the key-note of modern Science; and upon this orderliness of Nature scientific thinking is based. Hence, the much abused phrases "human liberty" and "human freedom" cannot imply anarchy or chaos, i. e. dis-order.

Liberty means absence of irrational restraint.

Freedom of thought can have but self-imposed limitations.

Social Freedom simply means liberty for rational individual activity tending to the accomplishment of Community Purpose.

National Self-determination.

When a Nation—exercising its freedom of choice—discards Autocracy and selects Democracy as its social principle it cannot successfully retain the working elements of the discarded social organization. If it is to survive, it must adopt ways and means and methods of life in consonance with its chosen principle.

Our Futile Experiment.

The United States, like a novice in Mechanics, has seemingly undertaken the futile experiment of building an Industrial Democracy out of the functional elements of Predatory Autocracy. The natural result is noise, friction and heat. And worse —a dangerously large proportion of our energy is wastefully expended in constant readjustment to keep the outfit running, and to prevent its pounding itself into scrap. Prac-

tically the whole of our "Economic and Financial System" is a left-over from the days when absolutism and privilege were universally accepted ideas and ideals; and when magic-causation was an unquestioned "fact." Quite naturally our economic customs, conventions and laws are in keeping with these antiquated assumptions. Substantially our "Economics" is a vestige, and as with other vestiges—like our vermiform appendix—it is now functionally useless, and frequently causes much unnecessary pain and trouble; which sooner or later may end in tragedy.

Not All Bad.

While, in the foregoing, there is no real cause for pessimism, there is even less reason for happy-go-lucky optimism.

Mentally reviewing this matter, t h e r e appear several implications which stand out clearly as definite practical suggestions for economic reconstruction.

Suggestions for Reconstruction.

First: That "chance" means ignorance.

The elimination of even the crudely obvious "chance" factors from our laws, customs and economic conventions, would do away with much rank injustice in our social functioning.

Second: That the onward flow of time is not reversible—the future cannot help the present.

A clear appreciation and practical application of this seemingly axiomatic proposition would go far to remedy the grosser evils of capitalistic economics, and strip "money" and "credit" of their conventionally endowed time-reversing magic.

In every physical human accomplishment, there are involved but three factors or elements: raw Material (Nature's free gift); human Time; human Energy. Every product (food, clothing, housing, transportation facilities, or what not), represents a definite amount of past human time and past human energy—gone beyond recall. Neither by ghostly hands nor by flibber-gib financial conventions can future work or future product be yanked back into the present, to be used for present purposes, or to meet

present emergencies—even if self-re-
spect and common honesty did not suffice to prevent such inexcusable cam-
ouflaged robbery of the helpless, the
quintessence of "taxation without representation."

Third: That cause-and-effect, not
whim, is the order of Nature's processes.

Science shows us that, so far as Man
is concerned, Nature is infinite potentialities; potentialities realizable in
terms of individual and collective purposes. We can if we will—providing
our aims and objectives are in accord
with the Rational Order of Nature.

It is only in purposive action that
human freedom—self-determination—
is expressed.

An aimless man or a purposeless
"nation" is an equally insignificant
fragment of raw material in Nature's
Evolutionary and Devolutionary processes. But, knowledge of Nature and
of Nature's Laws co-ordinated by Hu-

man Intelligence in rationally purposive actions, have all of Nature's infinite potentialities and stupendous
forces as tools to facilitate accomplishment.

Purposive Co-ordination.

Obviously the control of our Great
National Workshop—the United States
—should not be in the hands
of selfish Mr. Acquisitive Cunning—
"who knows the price of everything
and the value of nothing"—facile only
in getting something for nothing—and
whose highest social ideal is: "To buy
cheap and sell dear"; but—in reason,
in common horse sense!—our purposive Industrial Democracy should be
guided and directed by nationally organized and co-ordinated specialists in
all the branches of Skill, Technology,
and Science which are involved in its
Social Life and requisite to the suc-
cessful accomplishment of its Great
National Objective.

Fernwald, Berkeley, February, 1919.

IS THE ONWARD FLOW OF TIME REVERSIBLE
BY HUMAN CONVENTION?

Technocracy

PART IV.

Skill Economics for Industrial Democracy.

By William Henry Smyth

Note—In the previous essays of this series the author shows that men's characterizing activities express certain instincts or instinctive urges and that human societies (nations) today consist of uncoordinated groups, each bent upon gratifying its predominating instinctive urge—at the expense of other groups and regardless of the common weal.   He proposes as a remedy for this social strife a plan of National Co-ordination—Technocracy.

This article discusses some of the important phases more in detail, with constructive suggestions for the elimination of "chance," "mystery," and "magic" from our present economic processes, the substitution of intelligent purposive ways and means for haphazard methods; and for self-interested autocratic control, the substitution of Scientific Leadership organized for the accomplishment of consensus National Objectives.—Editor

Our Nationwide Machine Shop.

Attempting to make a robust man conform to nursery usages and swaddling clothes conventions would be no more absurd than our present efforts to conduct Twentieth Century life on the Hunter and Sheepherder customs of our racial infancy.

Indeed, it would be less preposterous than our continued efforts (despite tragic experience) to have lawyers and gamblers run our nationwide Machine Shop by methods and under conventions not differing essentially from ancient Babylonish laws of King Hamurabi and economic customs in vogue two thousand years before Christ.

Childish Economics.

Human society started with Bruteforce Economics, suitable to Caveman—Hunter and Fighter — times. Then humanity advanced through the Pastoral—animal breeder—stage, being therein confronted, socially and economically, with the awe-inspiring marvel of phallic phenomena, the fearful mystery of Death and the joy-inciting miracle of Life—life with its seemingly endless sequence of production and reproduction.

The Animal Breeder stage of development, indeed, seems to have left an indelible impression; seems to have peculiarly influenced man's mental outlook and modified his thinking processes so profoundly as to have

shaped even our modern business conventions and daily practices—or at least to have provided favorable psychic habitat for our conventional economic irrationalities.

Mysticism and Symbolism.

The mind-staggering miracle of generation seems to have thrown primitive human thinking back upon itself in dazed befogment—bewilderment and mistunderstanding of Nature's laws, out of which confusion of thought emerged Mysticism with its magic symbolism.

This mental chaos of mystic symbolism—the endowment of the symbol (or "representative") with the qualities and functions of the thing symbolized—is a primordial explanatory perversion which still characterizes our commonplace thinking on monetary matters.   The "power of money" is proverbial among us; and that "money makes money" is axiomatic to the average man; also that "money makes the mare go," and that it performs many other strenuously animistic stunts.

Money, Mortgages and Nehemiah.

Down through the ages occasionally we find (both in ecclesiastic and lay writings) clearly reasoned reprobation of practices based upon this naive misinterpretation of the facts of Nature.

"The words of Nehemiah, the son of Hacaliah" and cup bearer of Artaxerxes, king of Persia, are as "modern" today as on the day they were uttered—nearly five hundred years before Christ.

And they are as applicable to the "civilized" world today as they were to the kindergarten usages and antisocial practices of our civilization's nursery—Mesopotamia.

"Some also there were that said, We are mortgaging our fields and our vineyards, and our houses: let us get corn, because of the dearth. There were some also that said, We have borrowed money for the king's tribute upon our fields and our vineyards. Yet now our flesh is as the flesh of our brethren, our children as their children: and lo, we bring into bondage our sons and our daughters to be servants, and some of our daughters are brought into bondage already; neither is it in our power to help it; for other men have our fields and our vineyards.

"And I was very angry when I heard their cry and these words.

"Then I consulted with myself, and contended with the nobles and the rulers, (or deputies) and said unto them, Ye exact usury, every one of his brother. And I held a great assembly against them.

"And I said unto them, We after our ability have redeemed our brethren the Jews, which were sold unto the heathen; and would ye even sell your brethren? and should they be sold unto us?

"Then held they their peace, and found never a word.

"Also I said, The thing that ye do is not good:

"And I likewise, my brethren and my servants, do lend them money and corn on usury. I pray you let us leave off this usury.

"Restore, I pray you, to them, even this day, their fields, their vineyards, their olive yards, and their houses, also the hundredth part of the money, and of the corn, the wine, and the oil, that ye exact of them.

"Then said they, We will restore them, and require nothing of them; so will we do, even as thou sayest.

"Then I called the priests, and took an oath of them, that they should do according to this promise.

Also I shook out my lap, and said

So God shake out every man from his house, and from his labor, that performeth not this promise; even thus be he shaken out, and emptied.

"And all the congregation said, Amen, and praised the Lord.

"And the people did according to this promise." (Nehemiah Chap. 5.)

Money, Reason and Rome.

Practical minded ancient Rome, from whom we have learned so much of our work-a-day jurisprudence—while retaining many other gross superstitions—seems to have rejected this animistic pecuniary absurdity, as is shown by the familiar expression: Money does not procreate money — "Nummus nummum non parit."

Money, Sheep and Shylock.

The genius of Shakespeare realized the fatuity of this pastoral-age-founded pecuniary delusion that "money breeds money" (which still obsesses our misbegotten finance conventions), and holds it up to deserved ridicule:

(The Merchant of Venice—Act 1 Scene 3.)

Shylock:
When Jacob grazed his uncle Laban's sheep—

Antonio:
And what of him? Did he take interest?

Shylock:
No, not take interest, not, as you would say,
Directly interest: mark what Jacob did.
When Laban and himself were compromised
That all the eanlings which were streaked and pied
Should fall as Jacob's hire, the ewes, being rank,
In the end of autumn turned to the rams,
And, when the work of generation was
Between these woolly breeders in the act,
The skilful shepherd peel'd me certain wands
And, in the doing of the deed of kind,
He stuck them up before the fulsome ewes,
Who then conceiving did in eaning time

Fall parti-colored lambs, and those
were Jacob's.
This was a way to thrive, and he
was blessed:
And thrift is blessing, if men steal
it not.

Antonio:
. This was a venture, sir, that Jacob
served for;
A thing not in his power to bring
to pass,
But sway'd and fashion'd by the
hand of heaven.
Was this inserted to make interest
good?
Or is your gold and silver ewes
and rams?

Shylock:
I cannot tell; I make it breed as fast:

Adolescent Economics.

Magic-Mystery tinged Breeder-
economics and vocational experience
(misinterpreted) quite naturally resulted in Theocracy and Theocratic-
economics; and from Theocracy the
course is straight, the steps easy and
obvious to Working-by-proxy social
systems — Privilege-economics — as
represented by Autocracy, Aris-
tocracy, and modern Plutocracy.

Thus the race has successively
adopted Strength-economics, Cunning-economics, and Cunning-Strong-
economics; each system appropriate
to the conditions of life and stage
of development, in the past.

Adult Economics.

Today is the day of Doer, Worker, Maker—practical utilizer of
Nature by skill of hand and science-
taught brain—the Mechanic.

This is an age of applied Science—
the utilization of Nature's Laws and
forces — consequently the earlier
mystic, predatory, and parasitic
economic usages and conventions are
now antiquated and impracticable.
Hence they are beginning to revolt
our science-developed practical common sense, our sense of propriety,
and our modern sense of justice.

Furthermore, it is significantly in
accord with race experience, with
commonsense and with reason that:
Those whose activities characterize
the times, must initiate and administer its economics.

So if our Mechanistic Age, our
Democratic Dispensation is not to

prove a futile race experiment, a
will-o-the-wisp ideal, we must initiate Skill-economics, economics of
our Twentieth Century mechanis-
tically characterized activities—economics of the Scientist, of the Technologist, of the Mechanic, on a
nationwide scale, in other words:
National Industrial Management—
Technocracy.

Skill Economics.

The Mechanic's philosophy assumes: the neutral orderliness of
Nature; personal freedom; and personal responsibility for the outcome
of his acts.

The Mechanic's practice is based
upon: personal initiative; self- reli-
ance; and the validity of experience.

The Mechanic's success results
from: knowledge of Nature's laws;
experimental proof; and the elimination of "chance."

It is reasonable, therefore, to
assume that upon these fundamentals
also must be framed our new work-
a-day Skill-economics, in order to be
workable in our work-a-day Mechanistic Age.

As applied to our present obsolescent economics these principles
imply:

Elimination of Magic (as a tacitly
assumed factor) in the means and
methods of production.

Elimination of Mystery from our
means and methods of exchanging
human efforts and resulting products.

Elimination of Chance from industrial organization and distribution.

Twixt Devil and Deep Sea.

Stated as generalities, few will
question the desirability of such
changes; for it will readily be con-
ceded that "chance," "mystery," and
"magic" are merely expressions of
ignorance clothed in old and familiar
superstitions. But, when one comes
truly to realize—not just verbally
admit—how completely magic, mystery, and chance are woven into the
fabric of our modern life and
thought processes, then the true significance of the propositions strikes
the mind with a sense of shock.

We are, indeed, between the devil
and the deep sea!

Radically change we must, or our

"Civilization" will go the way of previous abortive social experiments —Assyria, Egypt, Phoenicia, Greece, Rome, Spain, and . . . Europe.

But, characteristically, the huge majority of us would rather be socially damned in the good old-fashioned way, than accept social salvation through radical change. Yet, if human experience proves anything, it demonstrates conclusively that irrationality cannot persist in the rational Order of Nature.

Chuck-a-Luck Economics.

Thus it will, perchance, be helpful to indicate some implications of the suggested eliminations, by more specific applications to present social, economic and financial customs, usages, and conventions.

Birth, Marriage, Death, are the time-worn dice in our chuck-a-luck economics.

Birth, in surroundings of wealth or poverty—on Fifth Avenue or in the Bowery—decides whether a child shall be a Master or a Servant, an owner or a slave, a nationally controlling factor or one of a million mere "cogs," regardless of inherent fitness to the "chance" ordained position, or to further the aims of the community.

Marriage, under our quaint economic conventions, decides into whose hands shall be entrusted power represented by vast accumulations of wealth, regardless of the chances that the easily acquired wealth may be frivolously squandered or used adversely to national purposes.

Death, with sardonic irrelevance, plays skittles with the lives of the living; for our weirdly jocund "laws of devise" empower dead hands from the grave to control thousands of living men's activities.

Makers and Takers.

Under our "economic and finance system" to be born into our Mechanistic Age with mechanical and constructive traits—dextrous hands, ingenious brain, and irresistible instinctive urge to do, to work, to make the things which constitute our "wealth"— is to be fore-doomed by "chance" to lifelong obscurity, social impotence, and relative poverty; while to be born with instinctive acquisitive cunning and insatiable greed, is to be elected by "chance" to social distinction, wealth and power.

Indeed, it would seem, that of all the facts, circumstances, and incidents, constituting present conditions of human life, "blind chance" has irrationally been selected as the controlling factor in that antiquated collection of queer customs, quaint conventions and grotesque superstitions, that, with childish fatuity, we call our "Science of Economics and Finance."

Magic—Ancient and Modern.

To gage the folly of earlier ages by our own advance is an easy and vanity satisfying diversion; to correctly measure the ignorance and superstition of our own times is a hopeless task.

Thus we look back with smiling contempt upon Devil-raising, Soul-selling, Fountain-of-youth, Witch's-broomstick, and other wondrous paraphernalia of "Black Art." And yet, no essential difference exists between the old witchcraft, by which a "magic potion" added years to human life, and modern "financial" black art which gives everlasting life to inanimate "capital" and endows lifeless "money" with life's unique function—reproduction—so that "money makes money" for ever and ever. Indeed, of the two the modern magic causation is the more crudely illogical and unscientific; for while the ancient black art only purported to prolong life already existing, modern financial magic pretends to perform the still greater miracle of infusing life into inanimate objects!

Do I seem to exaggerate?

Then read what Economic High Priest Boehm-Bawerk says in his "Capital and Interest—A Critical History of Economic Theory"; says seriously, supremely unconscious that he is describing a crazily impossible miracle—a miracle, however, in which there is a substantially universal consensus of ignorant belief.

"And finally it (interest) flows to the capitalist without ever exhausting the capital from which it comes, and therefore without any necessary limit to its continuance. It is, if one may use such an expression about mundane things, capable of an everlasting life.

Thus it is that the phenomenon of interest as a whole presents the remarkable picture of a lifeless thing producing an everlasting and inexhaustible supply of goods."

Was ever gross superstitious ignorance or "black art" more crassly at variance with facts and Nature's Laws or the Sciences of Physics and Mechanics, than this self-filling "magic purse" of financial wizardry?

Time Turned Tailward!

If there is one fact in human experience, the validity of which is beyond question, it is that the onward flow of Time is non-reversible, the future cannot help the present.

We can change the direction of motion in physical things—back up a horse, a train, or a boat, or even in some instances reverse the flow of a river; but to turn back the inexorable forward march of Time is unthinkable.

To suggest shooting the Germans with future bullets and feeding our soldier boys with future food—substituting "future savings" (!) of future generations for present savings and present work, seems—to a Mechanic—like the insane imaginings of a magic-crazed brain.

Yet, these are the stupendous miracles which the "magic of finance" seriously purports to accomplish—for a small present consideration.

Do I seem to exaggerate?

Then read the serious proposal of Financial Wizard Frank A. Vanderlip, President of the National City Bank of New York.

"This war must be financed, not out of past savings, but out of future savings. Future savings are for the moment not available and some other device must therefore be brought into play. That device is bank credit, and this loan and subsequent loans will in the main be floated through an expansion of credit."

Truly human credulity is limitless—or the day of witchcraft and miracles is not past!

Futilities of Magic.

Never in one solitary instance, in all the hundreds of years and millions of sacrificial victims, did entrails of slaughtered animals foretell a future happening; never did any of the armies of Devils and "familiar spirits," invoked by magic incantations, effect any earthly result which would not otherwise have occurred; never was solitary grain of gold transmuted from base metal by the magic of the myriads of guaranteed "Philosopher's Stones"; never did any of these miracles happen—except in the distorted imaginings of the simple ones who paid the Magicians for their futilities.

And the poor boobs who "paid the piper" didn't know any more about magic then, than the average man of today who frankly asserts: "I don't know a damned thing about Economics and Finance."

"Future Savings"!

Recalling practical warlike Rome, fighting her world-conquering battles or refraining from attack on the augury of fowl's entrails; remembering philosophical Greece conducting her civil, military, and economic affairs upon the assumed guidance of similar irrationalities; not forgetting that in comparatively recent times, by "selling indulgences,"—dealing in "future savings," "treasures in heaven," i. e., "floating (super-mundane) credit"—and by commerce in other optimistic and supposititious commodities, "the Church" acquired legal ownership to over half of the land and wealth of England; not overlooking the fact that by similar supposititious means modernized, the Mormon Church of the Latter Day Saints has become one of the wealthiest and socially most powerful capitalistic corporations in our midst today; calmly and dispassionately turning these facts over in the mind, causes one to pause and reflect. Indeed, mentally reviewing this ages long and unquestionable historical evidence, one—embued with modern scientific notions—begins to wonder.

Questions and Doubts.

One wonders how "dollars" or "debts" can be magically endowed with life?

How magically endowed with "everlasting life?"

How magically endowed with the capability of unending reproduction? —"a lifeless thing producing an everlasting and inexhaustible supply of goods."

And thus wondering, one questions and doubts. . . .

Can it be that the "miracles of finance" and the "magic of credit" are of a piece with the ancient miracles and magic?—only, (in keeping with the h. c. l.) gone up in cost to the simple ones who pay for the "miraculous" performances.

But what a cost!

Distribution.

Science and Mechanics have multiplied manifold the productive effect of human effort during the past century, so that the resulting products and instrumentalities of production have increased in like ratio.

So the question naturally arises as to what disposition has been made of this great aggregation of National Commissariat Stores in the United States under our alleged "economic" system?

How have the "Financiers"—our book-keepers—kept tab on the "debits and credits"?

How have they (numerically less than one per cent) distributed this product of the combined work of the twenty million families that, in round numbers, constitute (the other ninety-nine per cent of)the population?

The Balance Sheet.

In round numbers the books show:

$250,000,000,000—"wealth";

$70,000,000,000—gross "profits"; divided:—

$50,000,000,000—"income" to the book-keepers;

$20,000,000,000—"wage" to the families;

$1,000—average family "wage."

Thus the balance sheet shows that the self-selected and socially irresponsible score-keepers—the "Financiers" —have apportioned the gross yearly "profits" of the United States National Industrial Enterprise in the ratio of five-sevenths to themselves and two-sevenths to the 20 million families.

"Business" and Instincts.

In the jargon of "Business," "the Financiers" "charge" fifty billion dollars ($50,000,000,000) yearly for "financiering" the United States.

That is to say: "The Interests" assess the People of the United States fifty billion dollars ($50,000,000,000) "interest" tribute yearly, in perpetuity, for permitting the people the privilege of practicing national honesty—and for the magic of (mysteriously conventionalized) "Credit."

In other words: "The Capitalists" tax the People of the United States fifty billion dollars ($50,000,000,000) yearly for permitting the People the privilege of utilizing the Nation's human and other natural resources—and for (the miracles of) "Capitalization."

In simple terms of human instincts: The Instinctive Takers take the Instinctive Makers' makings for permitting the Makers to make the Nation's natural raw materials into desirable commodities.

Feeding and Breeding.

The families must, of course, be fed and clothed and housed, and the children schooled,—or the supply of Makers would soon peter out.

For these unavoidable necessities the "Financiers" allow, on an average, a thousand dollars a year per family; a "bare living wage" in exchange for a whole year of the brief work-life (of twenty odd years), for life-energy irrecoverably used up in making the wealth; wealth out of which bare sustenance is all that goes to its Makers.

Worse and More of It.

Nor is this all, nor the worst.

It deals with things only, now in existence. And it refers to an apportionment of the gross "profits" arrived at (more or less) by our own consent.

But,—by the wondrous working of "Credit"—the "Financiers" have virtually pawned (in their own pawn shop) the whole Industrial World!

The "Financiers" have placed a perpetual mortgage plaster of at least one thousand billion dollars ($1,000,000,-000,000) on the work and products of unborn generations of the hundred million families constituting the "White World."

The "Financiers" have chained thus a $10,000 debt, paying "interest" tribute of $2.00 per day (for ever) upon the back of each and every family in the "civilized world"—a perpetual thraldom of debt; debt secured by "Bonds," by "Mortgage," by "Capitalization" and by "National Debt" conventions.

The "Financiers" have thus placed this huge mortgage debt (in perpetuity) upon future generations without their consent—the most stupendous case of tyrannous "taxation without representation" in all the dark ages long tragic experience of long suffering humanity.

What petty "Pikers" were the Shylocks of old Nehemiah's day compared to our . . . our . . . "Financiers"!

Crowning Paradox.

Poverty is the opposite of riches; debt the negation of wealth; bankruptcy the reverse of solvency; they are antitheticals—the plus and minus signs of human interaction in the world of "Business."

A modern man, by the aid of scientific and mechanistic instrumentalities, accomplishes more today than one-, two-, and in some cases ten-score men of a hundred years ago; so, despite war and every other destructive agency, production outstrips bare need today as at no time in the past.

The world is constantly increasing its total products.

Yet, notwithstanding these facts, the richer the world grows, the more it owes—both relatively and actually; the greater its wealth, the deeper it is plunged in debt.

Thus, under the regime of capitalistic "High Finance," is achieved the crowning paradox of all time—the acme of miraculous causation:

The functions of plus and minus are reversed; more is less! The larger a thing grows the smaller it becomes! The more efficient men get, the less effective relatively is the outcome! The faster the world cistern is filled with wealth the more nearly empty it is,—the more completely is the White World bankrupt!!

The ancient miracle of "the widow's cruse" is inverted—by modern Financial Magic.

An Old Delusion.

Now it is not intended to impute deliberately dishonest or intentionally unethical methods to our Financiers and Capitalists, under a vague and metaphorical term, "Magic." On the contrary, I use the word "magic" in its ordinary meaning—supernatural effects.

I am convinced that the great majority of us—capitalist and laborer alike—are still obsessed with the fallacy of magic causation; an ancient delusion that has dominated men's minds and befogged their thinking from the very beginning of man's efforts to explain the causes of unusual happenings.

"Magic" is the oldest and easiest way to account for strange things, and still holds its ancient sway over men's minds outside the laboratory of the scientist and the workshop of the mechanic.

Elimination of this fallacy as a controlling factor in the distribution of products—wealth—is a necessary step toward a rationally workable economic system; a system adapted to 20th Century life and the mental attitude of our science-made Mechanistic Age.

Mystery.

"Chance" implies insufficient knowledge of causes.

"Magic" implies misinterpretation of causes.

"Mystery" implies inherent unknowableness of causes.

While increasing knowledge tends ever toward minimizing the "chance" element and lessening of "magic" errors, mystery presents a different problem.

The laboratory, or the factory, or the workshop, or the countinghouse, is no place for "mystery," for to the workers therein mystery means ignorance—lack of intelligence. In human life at large, it is quite otherwise as concerns the essential All-inclusive Mystery and religious mysticism. This is a fact of profound significance in relation to the larger aspect of our "Social Problem."

Our new Skill Economics, therefore, may not discourage man's innate love of mystery,—his inborn religious spirituality — nor curb the spirit which tempts him to adventure courageously into the unknown; but instead should provide advantageous scope for its personal expression.

But—as in the machine shop—"mystery" is out of place in finance; out of place because the function of "money" in an economic system corresponds to the purposes of checks and gauges, templets and measuring instruments of the technologist and the mechanical constructor.

The essentials of such devices are accuracy, certainty, invariability—the antitheses of the qualities of mystery.

Yet in no branch of human activity are its measuring devices so inconsistent, contradictory, inaccurate; so mysteriously variable, so subject to anti-social self-interested control as are those of the Financier—his twin mysteries, "Money" and "Credit."

Our Queer Dollar.

One of the many quaint functions of the dollar is that of a "standard of value." As a matter of fact, no one knows or can determine from moment to moment, what is the value of a dollar. We only know that its worth is diminishing, variously, to the vanishing point.

Neither the Nation nor the Monetary Experts, nor the Professors of Economics, nor the Financiers, nor the Interests, nor the Capitalists, nor the Common Man, have ever succeeded in fixing our "standard of value"—standardizing the value of our "standard of value"—the worth of our Dollar.

Mr. Worker contends that the contraction of the dollar is due to expansion in the cost of living; so he strikes for more dollars, and effects another shrink. Mr. Trader says the contraction is due to the expansion of wages; so he boosts up the price of products, and effects still another contraction. And so on and on, and the end is not yet!

Indeed, there are as many different explanations of this mysterious "spooky" phenomenon in our "Standard" almost as there are explainers—and their number is legion.

An Elastic Foot Rule!

If our foot-rule were subject to similar mysterious fluctuations, its length would have shrunk to four inches or so (!) in the past five years, with innumerable variations from time to time.

Imagine the chaos, had such a mysteriously variable standard of measurement been used in the machine shop!

The stress of War conditions has so completely demonstrated the inutility of our mysteriously elastic so-called "standard of value and medium of exchange" that it is now virtually in the discard,—stacked up uselessly in private and in national treasury vaults.

Our alleged "standard of value and medium of exchange" never was a standard of value, and now it is not even a medium of exchange. Quaint, but true!

A practically costless, hence unvarying, "medium of exchange"—a one-function money—is another much needed step toward a rational economic system.

Credit.

But if our money is a mysterious commodity, what shall be said of "Credit"?

"Money"—i.e., "gold coin of the United States of the present standard of weight and fineness"—even though lacking in practical utility, is at least a physical commodity. It occupies space (however uselessly); it has color, weight, length, breadth and thickness,—it possesses physical characteristics easily determinable by scientific tests.

Not one of these facts is applicable to "Credit."

"Credit" is a state of mind, a psychological condition—hypnosis—a mesmeric dream. Naturally it lacks all the qualities of physical things, and possesses all those of phantasms. A man dreams he is wealthy, and—for all dream purposes—he is wealthy; even though in actual fact he is dying of starvation in squalor and want.

So too, in like manner, a nation dreams itself some (or many) billions of additional wealth; sets the printing presses going to record the dream—in "bonds"; and forthwith becomes billions wealthier (in its mind), though, as a matter of fact, the physical wealth may have shrunk to the danger point of general indigence and starvation.

This is the danger-fraught "World condition" today.

Boundless Credit Wealth

Seemingly human stupidity is limitless and human credulity infinite! This boundless, unweighable, unmeasurable, hope-created dream-stuff ("Credit") is sliced and apportioned, like beef or butter, and sold in the market place by self-appointed purveyors of public optimism.

Yes! Sold and exchanged for the limited, measurable, physical products of sweaty and grimy toil and strenuous human effort.

Like all other dreams and dream-stuff. "Credit" visions know no bounds but those of desire. Millions or billions or scores of billions—it's all the same in the wonderland dreamworld of "Finance": wish them and dream them, and presto! they exist. They exist: dream ships, dream cannons, dream food—iridescent wealth bubbles blown up and "floated through an expansion of credit." as proposed by Finance Wizard Vanderlip.

Dream Wealth.

It is not surprising therefore that in the wonderland of Finance this dreamworld's dream wealth "Credit" —as represented by "credit instruments," i. e., stocks, bonds, mortgages, national debts, etc.—transcends greatly the workaday world's physical utilities—real wealth.

But what is going to happen when we are jolted awake to the rationality of workaday reality, and dream visions vanish; when the airy floating credit bubble bursts—as bubbles do? When Germany and Austria follow Russia's (Bolshevik) example, and France follows Germany, and then England, and then . . . ?

Then what?

When this happens, the world will discard the silly delusion that time is reversible by financial magic—credit; "credit," the greatest of all myths and magic makebelieves by which cunning men in all ages have sought to get something for nothing.

In all the historically recorded cases of collective human delusions—from practical Rome's entrail augury to shrewd Yankee Salem's witchcraft—there is none which surpasses, in collective crass credulity, our great Credit Myth!

A national (non-tribute) bookkeeping system equitably to determine real ownership of the products of effort, is a much needed economic convenience.

Experimental Science.

It would seem that with the advent of Experimental Science occurred an epoch in the history of our Race: an epochal event to which none other is comparable, except possibly the acquisition of Self-consciousness itself. Indeed it would seem that these two super-significant events—so unthinkably far apart in time—are, in essence, closely related.

By coming to Self-consciousness the Brute became Man—potentially, though not actually, a self-determining being.

By the coming of Science—based upon the idea of the rationality and neutrality of "nature"—potential Freedom ceased to be a mere possibility and became a realizable Ideal.

To Make or Break Shackles.

Science and Technology are, however, but tools in Man's hands; tools wherewith to make effective Man's transcendent privilege: Freedom of Choice.

Groups of men (like Germany) may use these great instrumentalities to forge social shackles upon themselves, and upon Humanity the bondage of autocracy.

Or, they may use them to make human Liberty effective, as is the ideal of the United States.

Human beings, whether as individuals, or as groups, or as nations, are "free" — self-determining — only when purposively initiative; for it is only in purposive action that liberty can be expressed.

Freedom, then, means will to intelligent self-expression — liberty expressed in rational accomplishment.

"Reconstruction."

On all the foregoing considerations, our problem of "Social Reconstruction" on a scientific basis implies systematizing our great but inchoate Nation upon economic principles appropriate to an Industrial Democracy.

The basis of modern industry being scientific knowledge of nature's laws whereby nature's resources are made available for human use and enjoyment through the aid and agency of technical skill, "Reconstruction" becomes essentially a process of selective rejection of present inappropriate economic usages; discarding customs which unduly facilitate the acquisitive instincts, and substituting others which tend to minimize social obstacles to the freer expression of the constructive or industrial instincts—in the interest of the commonweal.

As industrial processes involve specialized skill and expert technical training, made effective by intelligent co-ordination, it is clear that a humanly efficient Industrial Democracy necessitates leadership by those who possess the requisite knowledge, skill, and technical training.

So, when we speak of Industrial Democracy, what we really mean is: Nation-wide Industry managed by Technologists—a Nation of free and socially equal workers, scientifically organized for mutual benefit and unified purpose—a Technocracy.

Suggestions.

By way of summary, a few of the more obviously inappropriate present usages which, seemingly with advantage, we might consign to the limbo of outworn social expedients, here follow:

(I) Discard usages founded on the autocratic idea of "the State";

Substitute therefor—in fact as well as in theory—others resting upon the self-evident right of a man to inalienable and complete ownership of himself; hence (in effect) inalienable ownership of the industrial product resulting from the functioning of his mind and body—limited only by others' equal right.

(II) Discard conventions resting upon the parasitic idea that (legal) possession is equivalent to production;

Substitute natural ownership based on making for conventions that legalize taking.

(III) Discard institutions legalizing "chance" as a controlling factor for the distribution of things;

Substitute therefor collective foresight based upon experience; and human need for instinctive animal greed —in the interest of the commonweal.

(IV) Discard "financial magic" practices resting upon the animistic fallacy that inanimate objects can (by convention) be endowed with life's unique function—reproduction;

Substitute others on the evidential fact that only human beings can make usefully available the things we call "wealth."

(V) Discard the "mysteries of finance" in wealth distributing processes—the private purveying of public optimism for gain and the "manufacture of credit" for sale;

Substitute therefor a community (national) bookkeeping system, in which figures clearly tell what each individual and each group has added to the common stock.

(VI) Discard institutions resting upon the erroneous notion that conventional symbols, i. e., "representatives" of wealth, "bonds," "credit," "capital," etc.—are equivalent to and can perform the functions of the instrumentalities they "represent," and can continue so to function long after the instrumentalities have ceased to exist or have become obsolete;

Substitute others making the use-rent of things, i. e. "usury," "interest," correspond to and be contingent upon the effective worth and the continued usefulness of the things rented.

(VII) Discard customs based upon mystic symbolism and the animistic fallacy that "money" can perform the functions of the life-energy or products "represented";

Substitute a costless one-function national check medium of exchange.

(VIII) Discard "business" practices based upon the anti-social dictum that: "one man's misfortune is another's opportunity";

Substitute therefor the proposition that: the illhaps of unavoidable social hazards and chance favors of good fortune should (in social effect) be equally shared by all.

(IX) Discard all institutions and conventions facilitating the functioning of anti-social predatory and parasitic instincts;

Substitute others tending to encourage willing self-interested co-operation energized by national unity of purpose.

(X) Discard the strife inducing institutions of group industries based upon the hunger-slavery idea of employer and employee organized for mechanistic human efficiency in output of products for purely private profit;

Substitute others based upon rational human initiative and development with the aid of all the resources of the Nation, co-ordinated for the commonweal under the management of Scientific Leadership to accomplish a consensus National Objective.

Save Civilization!

Whether these proposed changes are effectively workable or are only "visionary," "impracticable," "Utopian dreams," is, of course, debatable; but there can be no question regarding the truth of the solemn warning of Lloyd George: "Civilization, unless we try to save it, may be precipitated and scattered to atoms."

Responsibility.

That our Civilization is in danger of being "shattered to atoms," raises the question of culpability for the present ominous state of affairs, and hence of responsibility for averting the threatened outcome.

The Masses cannot be held responsible, for they are simply impelled by their instinct "to live"; they do not think, they do what is much more important: they breed. Their magnificent all-inclusive social function is reproduction. Hence, they feel—feel hunger, feel passion—they feel with all the vital energy of the race.

Thus, when social conditions become unbearable or threaten their vital function, they reflex with unrestrained ferocity against such conventional restraints to the natural expression of their instinctive urges.

The Skilled Artisans cannot be held responsible, for they are merely obeying the instinct "to make." Their mental activity is analogous to—and for the same social purpose as—the cycle of brain functioning that produces the mathematical cell of the bee, the carpentry of the beaver, and the nest building of the bird.

The Employers cannot be held responsible, for they only express the instinct "to control," the Mastery instinct—an urge which could not be satisfied unless others willingly submitted to domination. Their social function is to energize—to counteract human inertia—for the preservation of the Race.

The Financiers cannot be held responsible, for they only reflex the instinct "to take," the urge to hoard,

like—and for the same social purpose as—the hoarding of the squirrel or the honey storing of the bee. They probably are least imaginative of all. Their social function is conservation, the converse of progressive theorizing.

Typically, none of these social elements think; think in the sense of the imaginative pioneer theorizing of creative thought—seeking for truth apart from its immediate application to self-preservation—searching with spiritual insight for paths into the unknown to be later trod by careless earth-bound feet.

The Scientist is in a different category. Characteristically he lacks the instinctive urges which distinguish the other elements of human society.

But, it is his social function to think. He does think—he has functioned with a vengeance!

One of the results of his high-pressure thinking is that: "Civilization may be shattered to atoms"—or Humanity raised to Godlike heights, by Science.

While it is quite questionable whether Science, so far, has proved a blessing or a curse to Humanity, there can be no doubt that its potentialities in either direction are limitless. Praiseworthy or culpable, as the case now stands, responsibility for the outcome rests squarely upon the shoulders of the Scientist.

National Leadership.

Notwithstanding appearances to the contrary—popular unrest, growth of socialism, spread of I. W. W.-ism, the whirlwind of Bolshevism and other terrifying upsurgings of destructive Massism—the "Masses" do not desire to lead, do not seek "proletarian dictatorship."

Human herds have always followed leaders, like other gregarious animals· followed their leaders willingly, blindly, thoughtlessly.

The herd will follow till following becomes vitally dangerous, threatens its social life—hinders the normal functioning of its instinctive urges to growth and reproduction.

Nations have followed the leadership of Autocracy till starved white by plundering conventions or bled white by wars.

Nations have followed the leadership of Theocratic Mystics into mental chaos, and confusion of human ideals and social purpose.

And we today, with sheeplike docility, have followed Plutocratic leadership into a social morass of crazy financial conventions, till the raising of families has become an unbearable burden, an impossible social handicap; till the opportunity to work is a dubious privilege; till the future of the worker and breeder—the proletarian—offers only a soul shriveling bondage of debasing and inescapable debt!

Modern Manhood's Mandate.

The present "World condition" means only that the proletariat has balked, revolted, at this sordid threat to the sanity and the sanctity of Human existence.

The "World condition" is a World Cry!—a cry not for Proletarian Dictatorship, nor for Mob Rule, but for new Leaders.

The World demands new Leaders! Not new and more "efficient" slave drivers—Trust Barons, or Kings of Commerce, or Emperors of Finance.

The Modern World demands modern Leaders, Men! Men with ideas that rise higher than swapping jackknives—even in carload or shipload lots.

The "World condition" expresses this demand by modern men for modern leaders, leaders with modern spiritualized ideals.

Our "Social Unrest" is a demand for torch-bearers and pathfinders to social freedom of opportunity; a demand for leaders with luminous imagination to visualize our War-born Nation's desired Peace Goal; leaders with scientific knowledge to realize and actualize the rational aspirations, ambitions, and ideals of free modern American Manhoood.

Scientist
vs.
Auto-, Theo-, and Pluto-crat

While the Autocrat, the Theocrat, and the Plutocrat, are decadent products of outworn ways and obsolescent materialistic manners of thinking, the Scientist, on the contrary, is the most modern development of modern intelligence, modern ideals, and modern spiritualized modes of thought.

The Scientist is essentially a pioneer,

a pathfinder, a torch bearer, a seeker after Truth and Rationality.

The Scientist is the modern religionist, the priest of selfless Truth:

Truth which grows with Man's growth and luminously emerges with the purifying of human Intelligence:

Truth—that all-inclusive Something behind the ,physical facts of nature which makes for Right—for mechanical, for personal, for ethical, for spiritual, for social righteousness—the ultimate Unifying Ideal.

Truly, "the stone which the builders rejected is become the head of the corner": the keystone of the social arch.

Rational Leadership.

The Scientist is, seemingly, our one best, if not our only hope for Rational Leadership.

Then, too, the Scientist—by unleashing the limitlessly powerful natural forces, in uncoordinated, haphazard science - made instrumentalities—has got us into much of our present social muddle.

So it is up to the Scientist to lead us out; or at least, to harness for human service the science-created non-moral mechanistic monster that he has liberated.

Guideless and Aimless!

But if the Scientist shirks this great task, if he lacks the desire for, or the courage of, or the will to Leadership; if for any reason he evades this obvious responsibility, or is daunted by its obvious difficulties . . . then indeed, blindly plunging deviously onward—guideless and aimless—"our Civilization may be precipitated and shattered to atoms," and our Industrial Democracy adventure prove a World Tragedy.

Yes! the most pathetic of all human tragedies—futility.

Lacking: Purpose.

Our Nation of great expectations, of magnificently vague hopes and stupendous possibilities, (if nothing worse happens), will slump into futile pottering desuetude, lacking inspiring purpose to live for, lacking worthy achievement to work for, lacking worthwhile goal to strive for, lacking —a. Great National Objective.

Fernwald, Berkeley, March 20, 1919.

Technocracy
Second Series
PART I.

Magic Money, Money Magic and the Magician;
The Payers and — the Fading Smile.

By William Henry Smyth

Note: The First Series of Technocracy outlines a program of social reconstruction under the guidance of nationally organized Science. The Second Series develops, in simple language and with common examples, the working method, the ways and means proposed by the author for attaining such social order and contentment, and thus destroying the peril of revolution.

In Part I Mr. Smyth sets forth the antagonism, in our society, of ancestral superstition, obvious in economics, notably effective in finance, as against the modern point of view, enforced by Science and our every-day-life familiarity with and dependence on machines and machine processes—with the resulting social tension accumulating to the breaking strain.—Editor.

Mechanics and Economics.

Mechanics deals with things— things governed by unchangeable and unchanging Laws of Nature. The basic facts and principles of Mechanic Arts have passed out of the region of doubt or controversy—they are firmly founded upon the proofs of scientific experiment.

Economics, on the contrary, is concerned with easily changeable (man-made) rules and regulations—community usages intended to facilitate social activities. Hardly any two authorities are agreed upon the basic "facts" of economics, nor are these "facts" determinable by the tests of experimental science.

Clarity and Obscurity.

Mechanics and machines, to Mr. Average Man, are quite within his comprehension and understandable to ordinary intelligence.

"Economics" and "Finance," to Mr. Average Man, seem realms of profound impenetrable mystery governed by occult forces.

Important Difference.

The difference in our mental attitude towards these two departments of human effort, to which I have directed attention, serves in part at least to explain why it is that we would unquestioningly accept (as being brilliantly reasonable) a proposal by a "Financier," that with spontaneous scorn we would reject (as being obviously crazy), if suggested by a mechanic.

It is so easy to overlook the customary that this common happening is not commonly noted; nonetheless it is a fact and social factor of more than ordinary importance, for it throws light on social problems, upon the solution of which may depend our escape, in the United States, from the condition of Europe, particularly that of Russia.

"Future Savings."

Obviously (to commonsense), if workers worked in future materials or if soldiers shot at each other with future bullets, or if both toilers and fighters fed on future food, only visionary products and dream carnage could result.

So, should a Mechanic propose to us an "invention" intended to enable workers, feeders, and fighters to fight today, feed today, work today, and jag today on next year's or next century's materials, food, booze, and energy; we should tap our foreheads significantly, and murmur—"Wheels!"

Let, however, Mr. Financier make the same proposition as Mr. (Nuttie) Mechanic, and we joyfully shout— "Hurrah! for the Future!"; and hand our "Wizard of Finance" a thousand billion dollar blanket mortgage "bond" on the world, (i. e., "National Debts," and intra-national "credit" instruments) paying Financier 5% interest for ever—to "finance the enterprise."

When a dapper and dextrous gentleman, in evening costume—with convincing evidence of "no deception"— produces ribbons and rabbits, pigeons and poultry, guinea-pigs and goldfish, from a magic hat, we—undeceived— smilingly applaud his skill.

But, let Mr. Financier's learned co-adjutor Professor Economicus solemnly and lengthily discourse learnedly regarding steaks and steamships; sugar, shoes and psychics; copper and coal; jags, joys and jimjams; cotton, coaloil, and cucumbers; cabbages and kings, dollars and diamonds, quantum and quahogs—all that heart of man desires—spontaneously generated out of a magic hat of "future savings" (i. e., mysteriously conventionalized "credit"), we listen in respectful amaze, and hopefully hand our petty surplus present products to Mr. Financier—as a small consideration for the great and mysterious future benefits to be conferred by his wondrous creative art!

Such "finance" and "economic" happenings as these are so common, usual, everyday experiences that they pass smoothly by without any awakening shock to our intelligence; thus they escape critical attention. Nonetheless from these casual unnoted causes flow our social unrest and world-conflict.

Magic Money.

(a) "This war must be financed, not out of past savings but out of future savings. Future savings are for the moment not available and some other device must therefore be brought into play. That device is bank credit, and this loan and subsequent loans will in the main be floated through an expansion of bank credit."

Money Magic.

(b) "And, finally, it flows in to the capitalist without ever exhausting the capital from which it comes, and therefore without any necessary limit to its continuance. It is, if one may use such an expression about mundane things, capable of an everlasting life. Thus it is that the phenomenon of interest as a whole presents the remarkable picture of a lifeless thing producing an everlasting and inexhaustible supply of goods."

"Economics" vs. Horsesense.

Quotation (a) is the considered pronouncement of a foremost banker and a national power in the "World of Finance."

Quotation (b) is the deliberate utterance of a leading if not the leading authority in the "Realm of Economics."

Both statements, with practical unanimity, are accepted as expressions of Twentieth Century economic intelligence.

If quotation (a) is not in essence precisely the proposal of our crazy "inventor" and if (b) does not in effect describe the performance of the prestidigitator, and if both are not definite and serious expressions of (real even if unconscious) belief in magic, then words have no meaning and rational thought is a futile farce.

Should either proposition (a or b) come (in precisely the same form) from a mechanic, it would require no stretch of the imagination to foretell the verdict of a lunacy commission regarding his fate.

Modern Diabolism.

It is noteworthy that our mental attitude toward the Mechanic is practical, matter-of-fact, modern; toward the Financier it is "natural," subconscious, and old as the human race.

In this first quarter of the Twentieth Century, the overwhelming majority still persist in our ages-old belief in supernatural outcomes— something from nothing. Indeed, it is probable that not one of us is quite liberated from the ancient thrall of superstition in some of its myriad aspects. So deeply ingrained in the fiber of human thought is the idea of magic causation, that this is still the "natural" explanation of any strange happening.

Our common speech, our vocations, relaxations, institutions, (secular and sacred), are full to overflowing with evidence to the persistance of practically universal belief in sorcery, demonology, witchcraft, black-art and magic.

We legalize "chance" for the distribution of wealth, for the "ownership" of property, and for success in life.

We commercialize and institutionalize luck, gambling, speculation —socialize worship of the "fickle goddess."

We pray "God" to pet and coddle us, and we bribe "Him" to clout without mercy those of whom we disapprove.

We supplicate rain for our little alfalfa patch—regardless of our neighbor's blossoming orchard.

We "bless" our friends politely, and "curse" our enemies with profuse elaboration.

We have sanctified days, places, and things, not forgetting a fair-sized remnant of super-sanctified people.

We habitually apply the term "wizard" to every man who produces results that arouse our wonder— Wizard of Invention, Wizard of Art, Wizard of Finance.

We constantly talk of the Magic of invention, the Magic of art, the Magic of money.

Still we ignore these facts and pretend that the modern use of hoary old witchcraft words is metaphorical, and that our continued use of Black Art and White Magic customs does not imply belief in Diabolism and necromancy as in the past.

But association of ideas, race history, nursery impressions, and community heritage are all too strong for the strongest of us, so the best we attain is verbal and vociferous denial thinly and shamefacedly masking conscious, subconscious, and unconscious belief in magic.

Two Ways of Thinking.

Add now the new factors, Modern Science and Printing.—with the concomitant spread of scientific thinking —which knows not, repudiates, and wars with mystery, occultism, magic— and we have the perfectly natural results which we see all around us: disagreements, disputes, strikes, lockouts, riots, I. W. W.-ism, Bolshevism, revolutions, rebellions, World War; results the final outcome of which— depending upon general human intelligence—will make for unprecedented social progress or for anarchy and the downfall of present civilization.

Mechanics, Modern Science and scientific mode of thinking practically began with the Steam Engine and modern machines of precision.

Economics is coeval with the Human Race.

So it has come about that each one of us has two separate sets of ideas, two distinct ways of thinking—the Ancient and the Modern.

Truth Resented.

Even so, a statement that our (more or less) self-consistent "Financial System" is to any serious extent constructed out of unscientific fancies and rests upon nothing more solid than ancient superstition, is a shock to vanity, as an insult to our intelligence: an insult directed not at the ignorant among us or at the thoughtless ordinary citizen, but, at our leaders and our teachers, and at the "brilliant intellects" that control the world's activities—the Premiers of Governments, the Kings of Commerce, the Emperors of Finance.

Nonetheless, I believe the accusation to be substantially true.

For a Consideration.

Under our modern business usages and economic customs, all social activities must be "financed"; every human purpose from "winning souls to God" to building a toboggan slide hellward; from constructing a "little red schoolhouse" to destroying an empire; from borning to burying, every human enterprise must (as a matter of course), be "financed"—for a consideration.

In brief, the modern fashion in

smoothly separating Doer and Maker from the desirable results of his doing and making, is by "financiering the enterprise"—for a consideration.

For a thousand years prior to our "Finance" dispensation, human activities and enterprises had to be (similarly) sanctioned by "the Church"—for a consideration.

For a thousand years or more, prior to "the Church," enterprises had to be similarly sanctioned by "the Oracle"—for a consideration.

Fashions change, but human nature is more unchanging than the granite cliffs; and the art of painlessly parting producer from his products is as old as civilization and—Magic still is, as it always has been, the painless parter's most effective "device."

Indeed, the art of separating the worker from the results of his industry is far older than the human race: animals swipe their neighbors' hoards, bears steal honey, and bee swarms rob each other.

Aeons of time and ages of human experience have not resulted in any essential change in purpose and outcome, but only in rendering the process more workmanlike and less messy.

Animism in "Economics."

A common feature in systems of magic is animism—attributing to inanimate objects the functions of life, assuming things to possess will, purpose, and power.

It is significant (though quite in keeping) that "Economists" and "Financiers" have this characteristic attitude of mind towards, and employ animistic forms of expression in writing and talking about "Money" and "Capital."

Whether this is due to unconscious belief in magic or is mere metaphor, the result, in either case, is befogging confusion of thought.

When the President of a great banking corporation, in a serious public discussion on "War Taxation," for example, says:

"Capital has a long memory . . .";
"Capital is proverbially timid . . .";
". . . treason for capital and capitalists . . .";

" . . . capital and men of enterprise . . .";
" . . . capital and capitalists of today . . . ";

he seems to be expressing nonsensical animism and belief in magic—magic no less crude and thinking no less naive and childlike than that of the average man-on-the-street in his oft-stated conviction that "Money makes money," that "Dimes breed dollars," and suchlike popular aphorisms.

Hazy verbal expression usually implies foggy thinking, and this is as true of the "highbrow" as of the rest of us. When language fails to clarify thought it is probable that the thoughts of its user need clarifying.

Interpretation.

Let us then (by means of a little paraphrastic amplification), endeavor to make clear just what our banker friend and adviser is really implying in these truly ear-catching phrases, which sound as though they really ought to mean something:

Capital (i. e. a spade, or a plow, or a crowbar, is more favorably endowed than many of the human users thereof—it) has a long memory . . .

Capital (i. e. a railroad, or a steamship, or a skyscraper is scared to be out alone after dark—it) is proverbially timid . . .

(It is) treason for capital (i. e. boilers and bullion, timber-land and mineral deposits, wharves and warehouses to preach and practice the forcible overthrow of our government) and (likewise also for) capitalists (when either capital or capitalist is caught in the act, he, she or it should be shot, or at least fed on low diet in close confinement until repentant) . . .

Capital and capitalists of today, (on account of their like human attributes, should be treated with all due and tender consideration of their like human frailties and timid self-sacrificing characteristics) . . .

I wonder if this is precisely what friend Banker intended to imply, and us to understand him to mean.

"Economic" Abracadabra.

The literature of Wizardry—and it is amazingly voluminous—is characterized, both in word and in thought, by mind-racking unintelligible obscurity. It is curiously significant that the books devoted to modern Economics and Finance are likewise couched in obscure jargon—abracadabra—not only meaningless to ordinary intelligence, but apparently also to the adepts in the alleged arts.

Here are a few samples culled at random from a page in an article on "The Nature and Mechanism (!) of Credit," appearing in the Quarterly Journal of Economics:

" . . . subjective value objectivised . . .";

" . . . force of value . . .";

" . . . psychic force . . .";

" . . . generic purchasing power . . .";

" . . . present good for future good . . .";

" . . . present value of future industrial worth . . .";

and the list might be almost indefinitely extended.

Truly, I do not lack courage, but I throw up my hands—confronted by these weirdly mystic phrases!

To me they seem as essentially meaningless as the twaddle of the March Hare and the Hatter that so puzzled poor Alice—in Wonderland. Subjected to mere commonsense analysis not one of these mysteriously cabalistic phrases seems to have any more meaning, or to have any more relation to actual things in a work-a-day world of Science and Mechanics, than the amazingly similar jargon of Wizardry.

Kilkenny Cats.

Practically every "Economist" writer invents his own vocabulary, and contradicts the statements of every other; they ridicule each other's reasoning; and seemingly each denies the validity of all economic axioms but his own—they fight like Kilkenny Cats.

A hurricane of verbalization has yowled and a flood of billingsgate has raged in this tempestuously wordy conflict of economic mysticism. Bankers flatly contradict Bankers; and Economists arrive at diametrically opposite conclusions—from the same "facts."

In no other department of human thought is there so much discord and confusion as in the "Science of Economics."

But . . . ! the Financier—gets there just the same.

Fact and Fancy.

It is practically certain that none of us knows when or to what extent superstition, ignorant mysticism and animistic fallacies color and vitiate his otherwise rational thinking. It should not surprise us, therefore, to find whole areas of activities still obsessed with this primitive mode of thought, nor that the actors therein are unconscious of their mental state. Would it not be the greatest miracle of all were it otherwise?

Thus it is in high degree probable that old fallacies and superstitions still infest and ramify (unsuspected) those activities which deal with life in its more than ordinary complex aspects—religion, philosophy, government, finance.

These considerations (even without taking into account the ever-present factor of instinctive self-interest) suffice to make probability verge on certainty, that all these departments of human activity involve an inextricable mingling of fact and fancy—science and superstition.

War.

Magic and Science—"Economics" and Mechanics—no contrast could be greater, no antithesis more complete; and between magic and science there must always be war.

Just as the World War—with all its variety of aspects and complexities of motives—expresses the inherent conflict between mutually exclusive and antagonistic social systems—ancient Autocracy and modern Democracy—so the world-wide social strife, industrial unrest, I. W. W.-ism, Bolshevism and other disruptive massisms, express, in last analysis the still more profound and equally unescapable conflict between ancient Superstition and modern Science.

Mumbo Jumbo.

One of the commonest of human errors is that of mentally putting the cart before the horse—mistaking the effect for the cause and vice versa. We all reason more or less childishly, impressed by the obvious.

In our childhood's games, custom (hoary with age) prescribes concurrent forms of senseless words and irrelevant acts, words and acts to which we ascribe such causative effect in the outcome that, to our childish minds, the game would be impossible without their magic.

So, too, it is much the same with us, as grownups.

In our social activities, custom (hoary with age and saturated with ancient superstitions) prescribes the mumbo jumbo we now call "financing the enterprise." And to our obsessed minds this voodoo becomes an all-important factor of such causative effect that without its potent magic it would be unsafe, if not impossible, to build a schoolhouse or wage a war.

Pedigree.

We see with our eyes the obvious fact that "financing" precedes and accompanies all undertakings and enterprises; we see with our eyes that doings, and makings, and enterprises grow apace and increase most marvelously, so—"naturally"—we ascribe to the "Financier" a large measure of effect in the outcome.

And the source of the financier's power to do these "miracles" and work these wonders being mysterious and occult, we "naturally" concede him a large share of the proceeds, and we (equally naturally) accord to our modern Wizard (of "Finance") that respectful awe which in all past times we have been accustomed to render to his forebears and predecessors in magic—the Medicine Man, the Witch Doctor, the Soothsayer, the Oracle, the Astrologer, the Magician, the Ecclesiastic.

Custom and usage is merely continuing its normal course in those two realms of activity now called Finance, and Productive Industry— Capital and Labor.

D-e-b-t Spells Slavery.

Enterprises (whether constructive or destructive, whether productive or unproductive, whether of peace or of war), when "financed," become indebted to the "Financier" in proportion to their magnitude; hence, the harder the worker works, the more industrious and enterprising the Worker Community, the faster and greater grows the Community indebtedness—a truly quaint, queer, curious and mysterious system of "economics"!

And the more closely it is examined the more quaintly mysterious it seems.

Mystery is and always has been the "device" of the cunning to despoil and enslave the simple; and no fact of large social significance is today more glaringly apparent than the general and mysterious drift of desirable things out of the hands of those who make them into the control of others.

Equally clear is it that the motor "device" in this drift, taken by-and-large, is that mysterious process we call "financing the enterprise"; and by the same token its most efficient instrumentality is magic money and money magic.

It is not necessary to assume conscious intent on the part of the "Financier" to enslave the "Worker Masses", still, in a practical world it is the practical outcome not the intent that is of practical importance; and in the orthography of modern economics "slavery" is spelled with only four letters—D-E-B-T.

The Magic Hat.

As—"economically" (!)—debt implies interest "which flows to the capitalist without ever exhausting the capital from which it comes and therefore without any necessary limit to its continuance, it is . . . capable of an everlasting life . . . a lifeless thing producing an everlasting and inexhaustible supply of goods"—steaks and steamships, welsh-rabbits and railroads, women and wine, dinners and diamonds, farms and factories; parks, palaces, pleasures, power—leisure and luxury, and all that lustful heart of man desires, all flowing in an everlasting, self-creating stream, not out of but into the magic hat—of the smiling financial prestidigitator.

But . . . ! the responsive smile

is ominously fading from the faces of the dazed payers of the performance, gazing in goggle-eyed perplexity at this quaint inversion of the familiar old magic-hat trick.

Who? and What?

Who are they from whose faces the smile is so ominously fading?

What does the fading of the smile mean?

What does it portend?

They—are "the people."

Of them I have written heretofore: "They do not think (constructively) . . . they feel — feel hunger, feel passion—they feel with all the vital energy of the race. Thus when social conditions become unbearable or threaten their vital function (reproduction), they reflex with unrestrained ferocity. . . . "

That is what it means—the fading of the smile.

What it portends is—Revolution.

Question!

Is that—even as only a possibility

Fernwald, Berkeley, California.
November 5, 1920.

—a worthwhile social outcome, considering our stupendous National opportunity?

Is our present social condition one to which we can justly point with National pride?

Is our present social condition worthy of National self-praise or of self-condemnation when we think of our century of nationally unhampered freedom and consider our vast continental area of the most fertile, the most resourceful, and most favorably situated land and—the most intelligent mass of human kind on earth, on the job?

Is our present social condition a goal for which an intelligent healthy-minded Nation would deliberately strive?

Is our present social condition the Objective for which we—as a Nation—have deliberately striven during our National life?

What is—now—our National Objective?

ANIMALS REPRODUCE THEIR KIND:
CAN "MONEY MAKE MONEY"?

Technocracy
Second Series
PART II.

The Method of Solving Problems Generally
And Our Social Problem in Particular.

By William Henry Smyth

Note: Part II of Technocracy—Second Series makes easily and clearly understandable a method of solving problems by disregarding details (accidentals) and focusing on principles (essentials), and the peculiar applicability of this method to the social problems.

In so applying it, it is shown that social forces and (human) materials are nature-given—unchangeable—and act in obedience to laws of nature (instinctive urges, etc.), but by the same method by which the mechanic utilizes "destructive" natural forces to subserve his human purposes, attains his ends, and prevents disaster, we may (and not otherwise) avoid impending social calamity—forestall revolution.

Freedom of Choice.

Nations, like individuals, have freedom of choice to do well or ill—to act wisely or otherwise.

Nations, like their human elements, are subject to growth, to degeneration, to catastrophe. They are subject, in other words, to evolution, devolution, revolution.

And, as in the case of individuals, their growth, health, freedom from accident—their continued prosperity—depends upon their knowledge of the laws of Nature and the intelligent use they make of this knowledge.

"Great" and "Small."

Seemingly "Nature" makes no more distinction between nations and individuals—is no more considerate of millions of units, than we are toward an ant or a swarm of ants.

Indeed, in the midst of the billions of giant suns constituting our "Universe" the significance of our whole huge Earth and all its contents, animate, and inanimate, seems to shrink into absolute negligibility.

But, "great" and "small" are human notions.

"Nature" is just as "great" in its smallest parts as it is "small" in its greatest. And it is human Intelligence which comprehends both the greatness of the telescopic universe of suns and solar systems, and the equal greatness of the microscopic "universe" of molecules and sub-molecules that make up a grain of sand.

Responsibility.

The practical point of this more or less philosophical introduction is that we humans find ourselves on a magnificently equipped earth, endowed with freedom of choice to use or abuse our splendid opportunities, with the inevitable alternative of sanely joyous life or futily premature death. And we of the United States hold the most favorable portion of the globe and an unequalled physical and spiritual heritage, with corresponding magnitude of responsibility; responsibility flowing from and out of our God-given and God-like freedom of choice.

Intelligence.

It is not necessary (as is both customary and confusing) to read "purpose" into the "acts of Nature." It is enough to discern their unmistakably marked drift.

This drift is a datum—a basic fact—that willy-nilly we must accept.

It is this drift we call Evolution.

But there is this distinction between Man and "Nature": Nature is impersonal, mechanistic; Man is endowed with Personality — intelligence and freedom of choice; and is thereby enabled to become an active and purposeful participator in the processes of evolution, and by judiciously selecting his relation to the drift he becomes the sole responsible arbiter of his fate —the master of his destiny.

Perplexity.

But, can man's finite mind really discern and steer a certain course among the infinite complexities of the Universe?

Why not?

The difficulty is not nearly so great as many think. For every complexity is reducible to simplicity.

Perhaps you have recently visited the California, one of our latest fighting ships. And being neither a naval man nor a mechanic, what you saw was probably a seemingly unintelligible and mind confusing mass of complexities, filling you with wonder, but also with helpless bewilderment.

Principles.

But, looked at the right way, the battleship would have been as easy reading as this sentence is to you. You would have automatically looked for the very few essential ideas—principles—upon which every mechanism and every combination of mechanisms must be built; and these perceived, the rest would have been as simple as unrolling a ball of twine; for, after all, what you saw was only a dug-out with cobble-stones to throw at the enemy—modernized.

Complex Machinery?

You know that the battleship hull is merely a large floating sharp-ended box or shell. You know that it has motor means to give it motion; steering means to give it direction; armament to give it fighting efficiency.

These simple essential elements equally characterize the primordial savage war-canoe and the modern civilized battleship; and so considered one is no more bewildering than the other. And both are equally within the grasp of common-sense clear and ordered comprehension.

As to the myriad minute details, by which these simple elements have gradually attained their modern re-finement, these are matters of merely incidental interest; each one of which complexities, however, could be reduced to the same simplicity separately—by the same method.

Indeed, these separate elements constitute subject matters of separate arts, and they have been arrived at by the skilled mechanic by a process essentially corresponding to that which I have suggested to you, as the right way of looking at the battleship.

Fictitious Complexity.

The Mechanic knows no more about the ultimate nature (i. e. details) of the matter, materials, and forces which he employs, than you knew about the details of a fighting craft.

All he knows or cares about are a few basic facts, the simple principles (elements) of Mechanics, and he produces his results, so bewildering to you in their fictitious complexity, by applying these simple principles to whatever task he tackles.

Experience.

You will not charge me with egotism if I remind you that I am talking as one who has been there.

In my long experience as inventor, as inventor's adviser, as expert in a multitude of technical questions and patent litigations involving matters of the most intricate character, I have never found my method of laying hold of the principles to fail; and I have never encountered another that will work.

Method.

Now this method, though unfortunately far from universally practiced, is quite universally available.

There is no reason in the world why you should not employ it as well, and with the same confidence, as I. For it rests, not upon a special endowment or any particular attainment, but on the commonsense discernment that every effect has a cause, and that at the bottom of a cluster of interrelated effects one must reach a simple cause.

Universal Applicability.

This effective method of attack is seemingly of universal applicability,

and you should now be able to recognize its use by me in the various.
articles of mine that you have read.
You may also fathom the cause and
foundation of the seemingly egotis-
tical confidence with which I, a
mere mechanic, plunge headlong into
t h e all-but-sacred-and-awe-inspiring
region of Sociology, Economics, and
Finance — and unhesitatingly invite
you to follow me.

The method has in the past enabled me to successfully pioneer in
quite a number of arts in the details
of which I was as ignorant as I am
of those of Economics and Finance.
Thus I do not feel that I am sug-
gesting to you a course fraught with
any more danger than that normal
to being alive: either when I recom-
mend your adoption of my method
of attacking problems generally or in
my asking you to follow me in my
application of it to our "Social Problem".

Why Pessimistic?

You will remember that the first
part of this series ended somewhat
pessimistically envisaging an ominous
prospect and causative influences
seemingly deep-seated and running
back into the mists of antiquity. The
great mass of the people are becom-
ing more and more discontented with
their condition, more and more per-
plexed concerning its cause, and more
and more bewildered (and increas-
ingly impatient) as to the course to
be pursued.

To all with eyes to see it is clear
that the social body is profoundly
sick. And equally clear, that to cure
a sickness, one must remove the
cause; and that unless the cause is
so removed, the sickness will run its
course—possibly to death.

Forestall Revolution.

In the social body, when the
process of sickness (such as we are
now passing through) reaches a critical point, another phase or phenomenon usually supervenes to save
the moribund body from actual extinction: Revolution.

And just as it is the task of a sick
man to fight off death, so our social

problem, in its essence, is the task
of forestalling Revolution.

Remember the California.

With our visit to the warship in
mind, let us now prepare to apply
to our Social Problem the method
there tried out.

We must first of all ascertain and
grasp securely the simple basic principles on which the mechanism of
the social body is built. This will
carry us out of the maze of confusing details into the clearness of ordered comprehension.

We shall then be in a position to
make an intelligent diagnosis of the
social disorder, and to at least think
clearly regarding the remedial course
to be adopted.

And, lest there be needless appre-
hension, let us note right here that
it will not be necessary for us to
lay down the curative (or reconstructive) procedure in its particu-
lars—"a practical remedy" in detail.
Just as on the battleship we should
find experts competent to execute
the details of any change found desirable, so we have in the social aggregation technicians to perform the
corresponding tasks.

What Evolution Is Not.

No word is more on people's lips
than "Evolution"; and none is more
frequently misused, and misunder-
stood.

Social Evolution is often talked of
as if it were a cosmic process forced
on men wholly from the outside, regardless of their yea and nay; or
again as if it were a beneficent dispensation "from on high" that some-
how, and regardless of men's acts,
will float them to the haven of social
bliss.

The typical expression of this
last extraordinary misconception is:
"Things will right themselves!"

What Evolution Is.

In so far as "Social Evolution" is
used not merely as a pretentious
label for any adventitious change,
but for a continuing process analogous to that which has produced the
animate world, from amoeba to Man,
Social Evolution is indeed a "Nat-

ural" force which Man must accept and to which he must adjust himself as to all other forces of Nature, but which, like any other natural force, is available to Man for the accomplishment of his own purposes.

Thus—and this is the decisive point —Man is not the helpless object of this evolutionary force, but a participating subject — a Master Mechanic.

Man's Will.

It is nonsense to say Capitalism must persist or that Socialism must come, by virtue of social evolution, whether men desire either one or the other or neither. Men in their social relations are not dust motes blown hither and thither by evolutionary winds. Men are intelligent beings, with freedom of choice; that is, free to use their intelligence.

Use their intelligence for what?

Obviously not for the purpose of trying to re-make Man—to treat as negligible basic traits fixed by successive survival through a million generations; or of attempting to alter the eternal forces of Nature.

That were vain indeed!

Natural forces, in social as well as in molecular and molar mechanics, in social as well as in biological evolution, are inexorable. They are not hostile to Man, neither are they friendly; they are simply regardless of him—impersonal.

If they have any "will", they show none toward Man.

But Man has will. Man has purpose.

Man can!—if he will. . .

Man's Way.

How then does Man do his will, work his purpose?

To him who tries to see below the surface it is clear that purposeful action invariably is pivoted on a judicious choice of the man's position in relation to the circumstances which he confronts.

This is true even of the trite conditions of our daily lives: even these are usually determined for us. Our real freedom of action means our choice of different ways of placing ourselves in relation to these con-

ditions—as a sailor, to keep his desired course, sets his sail with reference to the wind.

Choice of Relation.

It is even so with the greatest affairs, with the concerns of the Nation, with our whole Social Problem.

Certain forces face and envelop us that we cannot change. But we can set our social sails and order our actions in relation to them and thus mediately affect the course of our social craft in the direction of a humanly desirable, predetermined goal.

If our choice is unwise, those forces will run to our hurt. If we choose wisely, we may make a force seemingly opposed to our aim—subserve it. Thus we can convert what otherwise would have led to destruction into constructive upbuilding—change malefaction into benefaction, criminality into social service, general nuisance into commonweal.

Preventable Calamities.

Think of the Johnstown flood, the San Francisco fire, the Titanic disaster, the frequent destructive overflow of the Mississippi, the recurring inundations of the Sacramento Valley.

All these represent Nature acting regardless of Man; and Man acting regardless of his own intelligence.

In all these cases natural forces overwhelmed Man with calamity because he had failed to exercise his intelligence in rightly choosing his relation toward these forces.

After Event Wisdom.

After the destruction of Johnstown, the seasonal floodwaters were wisely impounded—to prevent a repetition of the disaster.

After the San Francisco fire, buildings were wisely constructed of steel and concrete and an adequate water supply provided—to prevent a repetition of the disaster.

After the Titanic and her human cargo had perished, her sister ship was wisely fitted with a double cellular bottom, and other provisions—to prevent a repetition of the disaster.

After seasonal floods of Sierra

snow waters have, time and again, destroyed, wholesale, men's works and the products of their industry, engineering measures are contemplated in our great valley—to prevent the recurring disasters.

Why Not Before?

The Johnstown people knew their danger from flood!

The San Franciscans knew their peculiar danger from fire!

The owners of the Titanic knew the danger from icebergs!

And all of us in the United States now—except those deliberately obstructing their mental vision with blinkers of happy-go-lucky optimism —realize our impending danger from Revolution.

There is nothing so foolish and ultimately disastrous as to blink unpleasant facts; "saying peace, peace: when there is no peace."

This blinking of facts—"trusting to luck", trusting that "things will right themselves"—is the true cause of disaster.

Shall we of the United States act like those foolish ones and like them suffer for our foolishness?

Shall we continue to act with equal foolishness and enact silly "prohibition" and other repressive laws intended to accomplish the impossible—change fundamental human instincts and overturn the unalterable laws of Nature?

Shall we, like Europe, wait to learn wisdom from social catastrophe—revolution?

I hope not.

Ways and Means.

My hope that we shall forestall revolution will undoubtedly be echoed by all true Americans.

But that our hope may be fulfilled, we cannot trust to luck or that things will right themselves.

It will be necessary above all that we act, and not only act, but act intelligently. And we seem, as yet, far from anything like a general understanding and agreement as to what must be done and what can be done.

We cannot (and we would not if we could) prevent the snow falling on the Sierras. We cannot prevent that snow from melting when and how fast it will. No matter how much we may prefer a nicely and "benevolently" calculated graduation, we cannot prevent a sudden and "malevolently" unseasonable rise of temperature and sudden starting of a thousand "devilishly" destructive freshets.

Adjust Ourselves.

But we can protect the forests, impound flood waters, regulate stream channels, build reservoirs, dams and levees. In short, we can forestall destruction flowing from impersonally-neutral natural forces, which in themselves are unpreventable.

Every one knows how much in that way we have already accomplished, and how much more is planned.

We are not, however, confined to prevention. Flood waters, which would devastate, can be (and, as well known, are) turned into priceless means of production. By intelligence and skill and purposefulness they are made the means of reclaiming for man's use the desert, and of "generating" light and power, and of helping to build up what may, and what many of us loyal Californians firmly believe will, become the apex of human culture, the highest and truest civilization on earth.

Immutable Nature.

The point of application is plain. There are about us social forces that in themselves are just as little under our control as are the snow fall and thaw. Left to themselves they must run their "natural" course. And, like as not before we have time to catch our breath, the flood will be upon us; that direst deluge of all—Revolution.

We cannot change the elemental facts of human nature.

Unchangeable Types.

In the first part of the first series of these Technocracy papers I have sketched in outline the origin and development of the primal instincts and propensities. These are as fixed as natural forces. They are, indeed, natural forces.

We cannot change a bellicose man into a pacifist—a Roosevelt into a

Wilson; nor a feeder and breeder into a philosopher; nor the acquisitive into the inventive. We cannot by any direct act abolish or even change selfishness, cunning, greed, cowardice, just as little as it would avail to try (and it has been tried) to eradicate courage, generosity, industry, public spirit.

Human Material.

To the social philosopher and the enlightened social reformer, and best of all to the plain citizen taking thought of these matters, the first step in the right direction, the first basic principle that must underlie an understanding of the present Social Disorder and be imbedded in the foundation of the Social Order to come, should be the real and effective recognition that all that may be accomplished must be accomplished with the existing human material.

Not Angels.

There is nothing in this proposition to cause dejection to any one except to those who think our only salvation lies in our acquiring halos and growing wings.

To many of us there is much deeper satisfaction and cause for hopefulness in the fact that, thanks to the Scientist, the Inventor, and the Mechanic, flying has become mechanically possible, than sorrow over the circumstance that our heads are not helioid and the skin covering our scapulas (male or female) remains as bare of feathers as before.

Reconstruction.

It is indeed the Scientist, the Inventor and the Mechanic who must, as I propose to show, guide and help us on our way—if we are to achieve social salvation.

Let our Scientists prove intelligent, our Inventors resourceful, our Mechanics skillful, and us ready to draw on our combined common-sense and courage, there need be little fear that our work of Social Reconstruction will be brought to naught by inadequate human material.

Reconstruction: That and no less we must attempt if we are to prevent disaster—forestall Revolution.

Simple Principles.

The obvious prerequisite to our beginning our reconstructive work is an understanding of ourselves and the existing social mechanism.

And to gain such understanding we shall follow the method outlined in connection with our visit to the California:

We shall refuse to be daunted by surface and fictitious intricacy and the multiplicity of details.

We shall seek out the simple essentials, and we shall remember:

First, that every mechanism whatever, no matter how vast and complicated, is built on simple principles.

Second, that it would be impractical and futile to specify "a practical remedy" or to lay down a "practical program of reconstruction" till we practically agree on social principles and practically agree on the purpose of the proposed social reconstruction.

Third, that laying hold of such principles is like unlocking a door; and a knowledge of the principles of the social structure is the key (and the only key) to an understanding of the whole of it and of how it works.

This last implies that it is needful also to note that to know how a mechanism works is as requisite as to know how it is made. Its working as well as its structure must be understood. But a knowledge of a structure almost certainly brings with it a like knowledge of its working.

It will therefore be our task to separate society into its very few and very simple main parts, and to observe their activities and the working of society as a whole.

Natural Groups.

Obviously the units of society are the human beings comprising it.

As I have set forth earlier, these human units naturally arrange themselves, by virtue of their economic traits, into natural groups. These groups, then, are the essential (main) parts of the social mechanism.

When we have learned to understand them, their interrelation, and their functioning—their natural working—we have learned to understand society as a whole.

Having learned this, our ideas regarding "Reconstruction" will have become clear, precise, and practically usable.

Unchangeable Human Nature.

Let us take a forward look here, in order to better know where we are at, and where we are going.

We cannot change human nature; on that we are, I hope, agreed. The human units are beyond the reach of Reconstruction.

Can we reconstruct their groupings—the social elements?

If I am right in holding that these groupings are the expression of immanent economic traits, and thus the working out of "human nature", these too are fixed facts.

The essential social elements are also not subject to Reconstruction.

What, then, in heaven's name, I almost hear you cry out, is there left to reconstruct?

Ask—Tin Lizzy.

If you had dealt as much with machinery as I, you would not be puzzled. And you will cease to be puzzled as soon as you reflect a little.

And—your tin Lizzy can tell you all about it.

Ask her, nicely and properly, she will tell you:

Her besetting vice is friction; but without friction she could do nothing—either praiseworthy or reprehensible.

Lacking friction: instead of being a jocund joy, she would be uselessly futile tinware.

She will skittishly skid on a greasy road, or stall in loose sand because of—insufficient friction.

But, also, she will refrain from these improprieties, a n s w e r her brake, and conform to your will only —because of friction.

It is friction getting in its deadly work when her joints and journals screech for oil; and it is friction that compels you to everlastingly buy and replace her worn-out in'ards.

But, and finally, she speeds her flirtatious chu-chu-ing way on the level and chug-chugs laboriously uphill—God bless her—by friction.

Freedom of Choice.

One and the same force, then, will work both "good" and "ill", depending on the conditioning interrelations—our selected relation toward the neutral natural force,—our purpose.

Just so, one and the same machine part, or one and the same social element, will under different conditions of interrelation or coordination produce totally different or even opposite results—depending on our choice of purpose.

In brief, what we can reconstruct is the interrelation of the social elements. And such reconstruction must proceed from a clear conception of what end the whole social mechanism is to serve—our National choice of purpose—our National Objective.

Fernwald, Berkeley, California.
November 11, 1920.

IS HUMAN FREEDOM ABSOLUTE OR IS IT
CONDITIONED ON RATIONALITY
AND NATURE'S LAWS?

Technocracy

Second Series

PART III.

A Working Method for a Workable Understanding
Of the Social Problem and of a Workable Reconstruction.

By William Henry Smyth

Note: Proceeding from the understanding reached in Part II, that the natural social forces are fixed facts which cannot be altered, Part III shows how they may be utilized for a human social purpose.

It shows that while human freedom must act within rigid laws of nature, it is not thereby limited. The intelligent realization of this fact has made the mechanic effective and his accomplishments possible; failure to attain this insight in social relations has produced what we call the "social problem."

Microscopic Scratch to Panama Canal.

Seemingly there is no physical task beyond the capability of the Mechanic:

Measuring and weighing machines accurately determining relations of ultra-microscopic minuteness up to those of cosmic magnitude; machines for production, for transportation, for reclamation, for communication; machines of all grades of size and of power, and of capacity, and of precision—from bolometer measuring variations in pressure of light-waves traversing infinite space to dreadnaught delivering its accurately placed and irresistible thousand-ton blows; from the hundred thousand in an inch accurately spaced diffraction-grating scratches to Culebra earth-gash of the Panama Canal:

These are some of the works of the Mechanic.

Methods Right and Wrong.

Clearly it is pertinent to our inquiry to ask: How does he do it?

When we note in one department of human effort certainty and success, and in another confusion and failure, it is more reasonable to infer that a deep-seated difference in method of procedure is involved than that the brains and intelligence of humanity have accidentally drifted into the one and deserted the other department.

The validity of this inference is emphasized by our common impression that Mechanics are more or less humble and low-brow, commonplace and ordinary fellows, while our Economists, Sociologists and Financiers are by-and-large haughty and high-brow, brainy and rather extraordinary personages.

The Mechanic's Wisdom.

Probably the most characteristic attitude of the mechanic toward the forces and materials with which he deals is unquestioning acceptance of the fact that he cannot change or anywise modify the laws of nature or the qualities of materials.

The mechanic, like the rest of us, wants to accomplish a multitude of purposes. Having determined upon the object of his desires, be it a machine to do something, or a change in the location of physical things, he proceeds upon the assumption which I have indicated: that he is debarred from changing or even modifying either the laws of nature or the character of materials; and so sets to work to get a clear understanding of these laws and of the characteristics of the materials involved. Then he so selects his relation to the appropriate forces and materials that thereby (through their natural cause-and-effect functioning) his purpose is accomplished.

Nature Dynamic

But, what do we mean by "Laws of Nature"?

We do not mean a catalogue of inert, dead "facts."

A law of nature implies motion, not rest—Universal Energy in universal orderly activity—it is not a static, but a dynamic concept.

It is the description of a process and the conditions under which it runs. Essentially it is a precise statement of the simple notion—based on experience—that if something happens, something else will happen as a consequence.

Nature is dynamic—it is eternal Doing.

Ceaseless change is of Nature's essence.

Even what we call inert matter is constantly changing and undergoing elaboration and displacement.

What does not change are certain relations, which we spell out under the notion of cause and effect.

Thus a law of nature is the expression of what is ever changeless within the ever changing.

Freedom Through Knowledge.

It is such clear and adequate understanding of and conformity to the laws of nature that gives to the Mechanic his freedom of action—his certainty, his success.

He goes to his task neither cowed by the irresistible natural forces nor ignorantly contemptuous of them. He knows them; and with his objective clear before him, he so makes his selection among them and so chooses his relation to them that his work may be accomplished through their service—through Universal Energy.

The Mechanic's purposive freedom (expressed in his accomplishments) is made effective through knowledge of, but by, Nature's Causative Activity.

Neutral Nature.

Nature is neutral to Man, to his hopes and his fears, his projects or his lack of them.

Neutrality, however, does not necessarily imply passivity. There is a neutrality in action as well as a neutrality in rest: A swimmer's choice of direction is not diminished if he can take advantage of currents flowing in the chosen course, but on the contrary, his effective liberty is thereby enhanced.

And the last word of Science is that "Nature" is an infinitely directioned but orderly flow of Universal Energy —currents infinitely directioned and available to liberate all who will patiently study them, and to realize all their rational purposes.

It is in this sense that there is truth in the otherwise inexact statement that the mechanic has learned to "control" nature.

As a matter of fact, he does not "control" nature.

As a matter of fact, also, nature does not "control" him.

Doing the Impossible.

Some of you will remember the time, not so very, very many years ago, when aeronautics was still in the balloon stage, and when at our own university here in Berkeley one of our most revered and renowned and forward - looking s c i e n t i s t s "demonstrated" that flight by a heavier-than-air contrivance was a physical impossibility — as contravening certain laws of nature.

As we all know, the Professor was wrong. But his error did not come from overrating the laws of nature, but from underrating man's freedom and ingenuity in choosing his relation to them.

The fact of gravitation is beyond the will of man and mechanic—leave it or lump it. It is just the same as it was when the Professor asserted the impossibility of the aeroplane. Yet now the overhead whirr (that still thrills some of us) has become so familiar that busy men hardly look up.

How was this seeming miracle accomplished?

In essence: by a design calculated to put the aviator in suitable speed relation to that proverbially lightest of things, the air, and thus its natural (upthrust) resilient energy counterbalances n a t u r a l (downthrust) gravitational "pull".

In short, the mechanic utilized natural forces appropriately—placed himself in appropriate relation—and thus attained his desired objective.

But, the mechanic, no more than the animal, the fish, or the bird, "controls" these forces of nature.

Conditioned: Not Limited.

The wind bloweth where it listeth. Of the forces of nature man cannot alter a jot. But he has practically unlimited scope for determining his own relation with regard to them.

Man does not control nature.

But man can utilize the active forces of nature—without limit.

The "Practical Mechanic" has learned this lesson, as he has also learned to utilize nature to attain his own objectives—hence his success.

The Social Mechanic (sociologist and economist) has learned neither; —hence his failure.

Considering the limitless extent and infinite complexity of nature, there is thus given to Man an equally unlimited scope for his activity—even to the point, as shown by the practical mechanic, of attaining the "Impossible".

This holds good of all men's aspirations and activities, in his social arrangements no less than in his mechanical contrivances. In one as in the other he has infinite choice.

Man may attempt the seeming impossible—and succeed!

Man is free!

What Is Freedom?

With respect to the laws of nature, and the mechanic's attitude toward them, may we not now feel that we are on firm ground?

But, what do we mean by "freedom"?

Freedom! Invoked by myriad-voiced chorus, called in vain by ignorance and folly! Spirit of democracy, yet not understood by democracy!

Endless foolish talk of freedom, with all manner of etherial attenuations of metaphysical abstractions, perfervid declamation, profound misconception!

What I mean by Freedom is exceedingly simple; but directly this meaning is grasped, the light it sheds on social relations becomes all-illuminating.

Freedom in matters social is precisely what I have shown to be the mechanic's freedom in his dealings with the forces of nature.

No more, no less.

Free to Choose.

The mechanic is not free to change, he is free to choose the facts and forces of nature. He is free to use them as he wills, to his own and others' good or—hurt.

Neither can you or I change the social forces, the social materials. But you and I and all of us together are free to choose and use them for a predetermined purpose and our advantage; but unused, they —with cosmic indifference — quite commonly run to our undoing.

The human units and essential group elements of the social structure and their natural laws are as much nature-given, nature-made and nature-determined, as the units, elements, and laws of the mechanic's constructions. They are the facts, the data which we must accept, as the mechanic accepts the characteristics and functions of the wood, or clay, or iron, or wedge, or lever, or whatnot of his craft.

The Only Way.

If Society and Social Reconstruction are to exercise freedom, it can only be by wise selection and purposeful utilization of the material offered by nature.

Chemist, electrotechnician, metallurgist, farmer, plant "originator", and animal breeder—all (in effect) so appreciate the rationale of their activities, and thus gain success.

When the stock-breeder wants cows that produce more milk or heavier beeves, he does not pray, nor employ magic, nor serve, notice of specifications on nature. What he does is to get busy with actually existing cows and beeves, in whose make-up he has no say whatever; and by applying his knowledge of genetics and crossing the appropriate strains, he finally gets what he is after. So far from "controlling" nature and essaying to dictate to her, he is her humble, patient and painstaking pupil. And so it is that he, after all (in effect), "makes" her do his will.

Let "Nature" Do It.

No one will more heartily agree with the Mechanic's Philosophy, as I have outlined it, than my friend Luther Burbank. He knows in highest degree how nature's "secrets" may be learned; not evoked by magic or any form of wizardry; not wrested by flying in the face of nature's laws or by nullifying natural forces; but gained by patient search, by persistent study, judicious choice, and intelligent application to a well defined purpose—objective. That is, exercising one's freedom in choosing his relation to the facts of nature. Man did not make the myriad-spike-armed cactus. But, Burbank has induced "Nature" to make the heretofore hostile cactus, spineless.

And so also, Dr. Jacques Loeb, Dr. Ritter, and the other biologists searching for the secret of how "life is made" and conceivably to "make" it themselves, they all, I feel confident, are imbued by the same understanding and in essence follow the same method.

Re "Social Problem."

This and no other must be our method in dealing with our Social Problem. Not otherwise will a (humanly desirable) New Order ever arise from the existing Social Disorder.

For this Disorder is the resultant of natural (social) forces, forces towards which men, failing to exercise their freedom of choice, have taken no defined and socially purposive position at all or an irrational position, i. e. in opposition to natural social forces. And these social forces will and must obey their immanent laws and run their nature-appointed course, even to the obliteration of civilization and civilized man's destruction, unless and until he becomes fully aware of the situation, learns to know the social forces and their laws which he confronts, and deals rationally with them as does the mechanic with the natural forces in his department of effort.

Let Man—in social relation—but reach such competence of insight and competence of action as the Mechanic has already attained and the horizon of the socially attainable will be extended immeasurably.

Scepticism.

It is not unnatural that so many proposals for social betterment should encounter scepticism. The man who waves them aside with the (to him) conclusive "'impossible," is less of an impossibilist than the typical "reformer" who makes them. For those proposals commonly rest, not on scientific knowledge of the natural laws involved and a competent technology in dealing with them, but on mere wish-father-to-the-t h o u g h t; f r o m which pedigree nothing comes but futility.

But a suggestion for social action, no matter how unprecedented, how "impractical," no matter how startling on the surface and to superficial inspection, if it discloses itself as securely founded on the facts and laws of society, will claim criticism of a very different order.

Only the self-interested will hurl angry epithets.

Only the unthinking will then cry "impossible."

Only the impractical will cry "Give us a practical remedy," "Give us a practical program of reconstruction."

And when the basic point of view which I am here abbreviatedly setting forth shall have gained acceptance, it will follow that what is now labelled impractical and socially impossible will be universally regarded as the matter-of-course; just as the "impractical" and "impossible" airplane of twenty years ago is with us, now, an every-day reality.

Absurdity Rampant!

If my extended experience with inventing had not taught me so securely that the most formidable obstacles and difficulties dissolve of themselves, as it were, before the method which I am outlining, and what victories over the "impractical" and "impossible" may thus be won, I do not know that I should have the heart for any sociologizing; so great and grotesque is the contrast between what humanly is and what humanly ought to be.

Look about in any direction: You

find absurdity running rampant—running Society.

Ubiq. H. C. L.

Charmed if not charming symbol of man's economic ineptitude—H. C. L.

Tons of paper and printer's ink and myriad dynes of linguistic energy have been used up in vain speculative efforts to track it to its lair, to stop its soaring, to understand, to curb, to control it.

And while the writing and disputing, learned and unlearned, are at their hottest,—lo! things mysteriously begin to happen.

Howls and Grins.

Wool drops 50 per cent and—a million-dollar howl goes up from the sheepmen.

Wheat, which sold at three dollars a few months ago, is now precariously hanging about two dollars. The price of cotton has been cut in two since spring. Cattle and hogs on the hoof have slumped. Prices of staple fruits are down—billion-dollar-shrieks from the agriculturalist.

City man grins.

Why Blame Anyone!

In the why of these ground-and-lofty acrobatic performances of "prices" I am not at present interested. But what does interest me—and you—at this point is the difference in emotional response from different portions of the American people.

Roars of rage from the farmer:

A nascent smile—a flickering grin —of hope on the faces of the urban consumers.

Would you blame the farmer?

I don't.

He must raise "high-priced" crops on his "high-priced" land—blessed are the land-speculators and boosters! How else could he make "interest," let alone a "profit," on his "investment"?—blessed our system of finance and financiers and "financiering the enterprise."

And is not everyone legitimately, necessarily, "naturally" out for the boodle?

Said a Hayward poultryman a little while ago (a very decent good-natured fellow, quite undistinguished for rapacity): "I hope eggs go to two dollars a dozen."

Can you blame him?

I don't.

Do you blame any "profiteer"?

I don't.

Would you blame Mr. City Consumer for rejoicing at Mr. Farmer's sorrow?

I don't.

Fifty-Fifty.

Let us note parenthetically that Mr. City Consumer's joy is, as yet, only anticipatory.

The decline in values on the farm has not, as yet, penetrated into his grocery store—with marked visibility. (Maybe it will not.) And his (decline-in-wool-inspired) scouting of clothiers' show windows has not, as yet, disclosed any hope-confirming tags.

Perhaps, indeed, though wool go down fifty per cent, suits may go up another fifty.

Why not?

Is not our "economic system" equal to almost anything—preposterous?

It "naturally" makes every citizen an enemy of every other!

"One man's misfortune is another's opportunity."

Of course! Naturally.

Serious Questions.

What are farms and farming to the city dweller?

What is the city man to the farmer?

What is the householder to the store-keeper?

What are they all to the laborer?

What is the laborer to them all?

What are producer and consumer to the Nation?

Where is there any understandable and unifying interest?

Civil War.

You cut yourself down to one fire in your house because coal is so dear; but West Virginia and Alabama have been enjoying the diversion of civil war, because the coal miners want more wages. And they are as far from sybaritism as you are from being a miser.

But the Coal Barons do not languish.

Truly our grotesque "economic system" is equal to almost anything preposterous.

Obviously it is equal to producing the quaint, Alice in Wonderland, result of placing one good and amiable American in Hayward and another equally good and equally amiable American in Berkeley into a relation of active antagonism in life and death hostility of interests and aims; hostility as real, as necessary, as "natural," as if they were members, not of a supposedly unified nation, but subjects of two atrocious nations—at war with each other.

Quaint hardly expresses it . . .eh?

Those Patched Breeches!

Why has wool, let us say, dropped in price?

Because, say the "economists and financiers," the world's market for wool is overstocked.

Think of it!

But how on earth has it become overstocked?

Think of it.

If a tithe we are told about Europe is true, half her people have hardly rags wherewith to cover their nakedness. And we dwellers in the richest land of the earth (and, as we sometimes fancy, owners thereof) have we not been performing marvels of skill and patience (ye gods, how long it seems!) in patching sleeve elbows, in patching shoes, in patching breeches seats, in patching our ragged tempers, and in pretending that—if we have one —an overcoat is appropriate for summer wear and—public appearance.

Why?

A sheepraiser in the Sacramento valley will tell you he is compelled to warehouse his present season's clip indefinitely.

Why?

"Wool is not now saleable"!— "There is no demand whatever!"

No demand for wool! Mark that.

And, of course no one feels the slightest desire for a new suit of clothing.

So there you are.

Truly, quaint beyond expression.

How do you like it, Mr. Man?

And, how do you like it, Friend Lady?

Futile Tinkering.

But these examples of our preposterous "economics" are obvious and commonplace. I should not waste my time and your patience just to speak of such trite matters; or to add another "practical" suggestion for "bettering" them to the futile scrap-heap of "practical" palliatives.

He would, indeed, be a fool-mechanic who would waste time and material tinkering with details of a mechanism after having on careful examination decided the device to be wrong in basic principle.

Why waste futile anger and energy on Financiers and Profiteers when they are perfectly "natural" elements in our "economic system," as our national social aggregation has developed from its ages-old "natural" heritage?

I would not, if I could, stop Profiteers from profiteering, nor Financiers from financiering, nor punish any one for playing our fool-game according to its crazy rules—better than the rest of us.

Effective Reconstruction.

What I am driving at is a working method, for a workable understanding of the "Social Problem," and a workable Social Reconstruction.

However difficult in application it may appear to the unthinking, or however undesirable to the self-interested, the method I propose has the effectiveness and simplicity of rationality. It has that perfect simplicity which lies at the heart of useful discovery and invention.

The discernment for which I plead is that our society is wrong in basic principle, is based on anti-social principles. It is a left-over from our European heritage and—headed for the same outcome.

Its various parts have developed in obedience to natural forces, are working in obedience to natural forces, and the outcome will be the natural result of the interaction of these nature-given materials and natural forces.

Elements Unchangeable.

It is childishly futile to try to tinker any social machine part—any social element—into workability, by itself.

In the first place, these elements are in their essential qualities unmodifiable. Just as the mechanic's materials are unchangeable.

In the second place, even could they be singly altered, what good would that do? They still would remain essentially isolated elements, aggregated in this or that connection, but uncombined by any unifying human design into a humanly purposeful whole.

Society a Machine.

It has not been effectively recognized, despite the universal use of the phrase "social body," that society is a body—a mechanism.

Just as a man's body is really a machine, a heat motor, as mechanistic as a Tin Lizzie or a battleship; just as an army (in every proper sense of the term) is a military machine: so a Town, a State, or a Nation is equally mechanistic—a true Machine.

Let us look for a moment at the effective implication and significance of this notion . . .

When your body is "sick" and annoying you by not obeying your will, it is acting in obedience to universal law with the same precision, regularity, and mechanistic predictableness, as when it was "well" and acting responsive to your will.

The only real difference is: in one case you like, and in the other you dislike,—the outcomes of the same universal law, the same mechanistic natural order.

Fernwald, Berkeley, California.
November 15, 1920.

Just so with the social body.

If we do not like the outcome of our social organization, and if we will use our constructive imagination to conceive an outcome more to our liking and use our freedom of choice to choose such outcome; and if we have initiative to undertake, and constructive skill (and courage) to rearrange the nature-given elements in suitable relation to social forces and factors to produce the chosen outcome—then the solution of our "Social Problem" will be in process.

And as I have said, "sickness" which in the human body brings crises, boding physical death, in the social body brings—Revolution—portent of National Dissolution.

Purposeful Social Evolution.

It is quite useless to promulgate "practical" programs and platforms, and childishly impractical to prate of the common interests of (dead) "capital" and (living) "labor" and the need of bringing them together, and so forth, and so on and on . . .

The only measure that will prevent Revolution is Purposeful Social Evolution: Social Reconstruction of such kind as will turn what is now a senseless anti-social, internecine warring aggregation, into a purposeful working combination; into a real Nation—a Nation unified by a common purpose—a National Objective.

IS NOT HUMAN PURPOSIVE FREEDOM
MADE EFFECTIVE BY KNOWLEDGE OF
NATURE'S CAUSATIVE ACTIVITY?

Technocracy

Second Series

PART IV.

Labor, Skill, Tally, Organization and Their Functions: Production, Distribution, Direction.

By William Henry Smyth

Note: This the concluding part of Technocracy—Second Series gathers up the preceding considerations for their logical conclusions.

The solution of the social problem is shown to lie in man's making use of his unique self-conscious freedom and rationality for purposefully co-ordinating the nature-given and nature-elaborated elements of the social structure; which the essay describes in their essentials. In this way man makes himself a participator in the miracle of creation, the evolutionary process, and his own physical, social, and spiritual development.

The alternative presented is, on one hand: animal instincts running their "natural" course to social chaos, to revolution; on the other hand: human reason utilizing the instincts, for the attainment of social order, true social evolution.

Basic Requirements.

Feeding and Breeding are the fundamentals of social life.

Any circumstance—"natural" happening, or artificial arrangement—adverse to these basic requirements is anti-social and socially disruptive. Conditions favorable thereto are conducive to social development.

Inherited Animal Instincts.

Not only are these requirements basic to human society, but they are and always were equally necessary to all forms of "lower" animate existence.

Thus it is that (to ensure feeding and breeding), "Nature" during the aeons of experimentation which we call "Evolution" has developed a variety of fixed preservative instincts, traits, and characteristics in the animal world. From the animal world, we as animals have inherited such of these instincts, traits, and characteristics as were necessary or most favorable to Man's survival and present dominance.

"Gifts": Peculiarly Human.

In addition to these, man has acquired, attained, or been endowed with "gifts" peculiar to himself which render him unique—Consciousness of Self, Freedom of Choice, and Purposive Rationality.

A Cosmic Invitation.

By these latter acquisitions, Man has been placed in the peculiar situation of being an invited participator in the evolutionary process, including also the working of this cosmic process as concerns himself.

This momentous invitation he is free to accept or reject.

Accepted?

If he accepts the invitation he assumes its inherently implied terms. He assumes responsibility for the outcome of his interference with the evolutionary process. He gets the benefits which his intelligent co-operation may bring him, and the accomplishment of his own desires, but, also, he must bear the pains and penalties of his own foolish actions.

If he accepts the invitation to take a responsible part in his own evolution, he has at his disposal all of the active forces of Nature including those which motivate himself,—his bodily mechanism, his instincts, his proclivities, his economic traits, his intelligence—to make or mar himself and his institutions.

Rejected?

If he does not accept the invitation to participate in the miracle of creation and the Cosmic Enterprise, the Great Undertaking goes on without a flicker of disturbance—indifferent to his existence—or what amounts to the same, regardless of outcomes which are humanly desirable.

Outcome.

All of this means that human society as it exists today is the end-result of these various factors.

If the outcome does not please or suit us it is our own fault and the remedy lies in our own hands—with the proviso that we realize the terms of the implied contract and understand the nature of the instrumentalities at our disposal with which to realize our purposes.

Conditioned on Understanding.

In brief then, all human accomplishment, all invention, all attainment of anything "new," are conditioned on an understanding of the facts and laws of nature involved and the choice of an appropriate relation to them, with reference to the determined purpose.

Society is a structure based, like everything else in the universe, on nature-given facts and laws.

The prerequisite then to our present endeavor, to map out a course of social progress, is to have a clear understanding of the facts and laws of nature involved: of which the first item is society's composition.

Elements.

Man is a strong, skilful, cunning animal endowed with freedom of choice. Some are characteristically Strong, some are characteristically Skilful, some are characteristically Cunning. In others, again, these basic traits are merged in varying proportions.

The Social Elements—the essential (or main) parts of society—then are the groups formed primarily by the working out of the instinctive proclivities which I briefly sketched in the opening part of the first series of Technocracy.

The Economic Traits, strength, skill, cunning and the instincts, to live, to make, to control, to take, have founded and formed our social structure, in which they are still recognizable as its four great elements: Labor,

Skill, Tally, ("Capital"), Organization ("Government").

Labor.

By Labor I mean that activity which is chiefly muscular effort. It is obviously the foundation of all other activities whatever, and as such it engrosses the effort of the great majority—the bulk of "the people".

Their motive urge is mainly "to live". They are impelled by no other special impetus towards any particular form of activity. Those who do the bulk of the world's work therefore find self-expression in the measure in which their work conduces to the satisfaction of their instinct "to live".

Thwart this, and Labor balks.

Skill.

Skill, expressing the instinct "to make", must be taken in a sense wide enough to embrace not only dexterity, but also usable knowledge of matters and things conducive to physical accomplishment. The Skill element of society holds the scientist as well as the artisan, philosophy as well as technology.

The function of such a Skill element in a rationally, purposefully organized society is self-evident. How woefully far from this it departs in the actually existing society is likewise self-evident.

Tally.

Whenever team-work is under way—or for that matter team-play—there is need of a record of each man's performance. To keep such record is the function of the Tally element in society.

This colorless, yet all-important, function the cunning instinct "to take" early made its own. The embodiments of that urge made themselves the keepers of the social tally-sheet—the "Financiers".

Organization.

The Organization element coordinates and supervises the work of society. It prescribes what should and what should not be done, in relation to the work in hand—the purpose.

This element embraces the "authorities", the "government", the "employers".

Necessity and Freedom.

The quality uniformly exhibited by all four social elements is their instinctiveness. They have developed from inward necessity.

But there is no such inner necessity for their interrelation, their coordination and combination into a social machine as a whole. That is not a matter of instinctive urge, but a problem of intelligence.

The present chaotic lack of coordination is due to lack of social purposive intelligence; it is the "natural" result of (and has been determined by) failure (socially) to exercise Man's transcendent prerogative: Freedom of Choice—freedom to choose his relation to natural forces in such manner as to make them subserve his predetermined united purpose—Community objective.

War of Instincts.

Indeed, each element, far from uniting with the others in purpose, is "naturally" fighting every other for a greater gratification of its own "natural" urge, and the all-embracing urge of instinctive self-preservation.

It is in highest degree probable that, typically, the four instinct-characterized groups of modern society—the Masses, the Artisans, the Employers, the Financiers—do not think. Thinking is not their social function; they merely respond to the urge of their dominating instincts—the Masses to breed, the Artisan to make, the Employer to energize, the Financier to hoard—instincts which characterize separately many animals other than Man.

These various social groups instinctively resist any social conditions or conventions that tend to hamper the functioning urge of their characterizing instinct and instinctively struggle for its greater gratification—hence our "Social Problems".

What Is the Social Problem?

The Scientists—scattered and few in number but socially significant—do think; it is their social function to think, to rationalize with constructive imagination. It is the Scientist's

function to solve problems, to pioneer, to blaze a trail into the unknown—to illumine the path of Social Progress.

Clearly it is 'the Scientist's social function to straighten out social snarls, to unravel social tangles:

To so organize society that human freedom and self-expression will be the product of and result from the rational relationing, the coordinate functioning and gratification of the human instincts.

That is the Scientist's great task. That is our Social Problem.

Purposeless.

Socially, Man has remained a merely instinctively acting animal. He has never unitedly pondered a social purpose, reflected on a freely chosen united objective.

When our inspection of the California had disclosed its constituent elements, we knew as readily for what purpose they were to work together: we knew what the battleship was for.

But for what socially determined end do our Financiers finance, our inventors invent, our laborers labor?

What is the purpose of Society?

Is it not true that, judging from society as it is, we must say it has no purpose?

Is it any wonder then, that we have a "Social Problem", and that most men face it in utter bewilderment?

Purpose Necessary.

To deal effectively with the social problem requires then, first of all, that men become conscious of a social purpose. And a very little reflection will disclose the enormous difference which a difference of purpose effects with regard to otherwise identical processes.

The same purposive skill that makes—feloniously breaks.

Bees and Profiteers.

Our profiteers have been filling their coffers just as bees are filling their combs. Essentially their activities proceed from the same source: instinctive drive to hoard.

Bee and profiteer are equally "selfish".

Each acts in obedience to the demand for self-expression. But whereas the utility of the profiteer's hoard (if it has any true utility at all) is for himself alone and prejudicial to society, the bee's honey hoard is for the whole hive.

What "Nature" has contrived in thus shaping toward an ulterior purpose the instinctive activities of a lowly insect, men must accomplish in their social arrangements by the exercise of their distinctively human qualities: reason, freedom and purpose.

No Use Calling Names.

It is quite needless and useless to single out the profiteer for moral objurgation; and in many, if not most cases it would be unjust to boot. His profit-gouging comes not from moral depravity, but from a special bent of mind, a particular ability: and our society, imprimis our quaint system of "finance," gives no scope to that ability—except to gouge the public.

Yet that ability—in its essence, instinctive hoarding—has a social utility of the highest order. And in an enlightened society, that is one purposively organized, it would not only find scope for its exercise for the public good, but be spontaneously so exercised, and with no less gratification for its possessor.

The War Illustration.

Of how this might be accomplished, the War has already given us a sketchy illustration.

The men who were called to mobilize the social forces of the United States were commonly the very men whose pre-war activities had been more notorious for amassing huge private fortunes than celebrated for selfless public service.

Between the high officials of the War Industries Board, the Shipping Board, and so forth, and the membership of a "Millionaires' Club" there was little discernible difference of personnel.

Charles M. Schwab, the finance magnate, and Schwab, the war-organizer, were the same person.

All these men brought to their social, national jobs the very same talents that they had been employing right along self-centeredly—unsocially, un-nationally. The work they did, their proximate functioning, was the same as before.

But what a difference in social result!

They were acting for a different purpose. That really makes up the whole of the difference.

The skill that feloniously breaks—can also make.

Where these hurriedly assembled mobilizers fell short of efficacy it was in the measure of their failure to equate completely their aims with the National Objective.

Greater "Temptation."

It is worth while considering how it was that men pre-eminent for capacity of self-aggrandisement, for their ability, to put it in plain words, of using the Nation for their own private aims and advantage, came to make the Nation's purpose their own.

The outstanding fact is that they did it of their own free will.

The deeper lying fact is that they responded to the greater inducement: public good was a stronger stimulus, a greater "temptation," than private profit.

The decisive fact is that such response was made possible and induced by the (even if only crude and temporary) rearrangement of the social elements for the attainment of a National Purpose.

Work.

Add to this the perception, for which I have so often contended, that there is no blinder folly than that which sees in "work" nothing but "the primal curse"; and that, on the contrary, doing—which is only another name for work—is the very essence and end of man's living, provided only it be the purposive work of his heart—and you have the whole foundation of the psychology of social reconstruction.

Order, Purpose, Freedom.

Freedom is the first law of Man's nature.

Any social convention or construction which does violence to the freedom of the individual, of the group, or of the Nation as a whole, is doomed to inevitable failure.

If any single cause is to be given for the social failure which we now so anxiously face, this cause, which earlier I have formulated as the absence of purposive design, may well be formulated as the infraction of the basic law of freedom. For in a chance-made agglomeration true Freedom can not arise and act, any more than in a void.

It is only in a true Order, in a purposively designed and rationally combined society, that Freedom can find the conditions for its effective being, its self-realizing activity.

Disorder—Jungle Law—Restraint.

Obviously there can be no real human freedom in a society based on primeval jungle law, only license and restraint. When it is the sole acting principle, (even if not the preaching of the pulpit) that he may take who has the power, and he shall keep who can, what can be the issue but intra-social warfare?—and, still more repugnant, a warfare in which victory is not to the strong, clean and courageous, but to the sordid, tricky and cunning.

Fictitious Freedom.

Let us not be misled by surface appearances. Ostensibly the mine owner has more freedom than the miner, the manufacturer than the mechanic, the merchant than the clerk. More profoundly, one is found to be as unfree as the other. For freedom implies doing one's reasoned will. But as members of a planless social monstrosity, no man can be a free agent. All are caught in the same chaotic social tangle; none guide their course by anything better than chance and their instinctive proclivities.

Reason and Freedom.

These instincts, as I have pointed out, are natural forces. And I have also shown how Man, the Mechanic, has achieved his conquests by bringing his Reason and Freedom of Choice to bear on natural forces: not in crazy hope of changing them, but to make them the realizing means for his reason and freedom—for his purpose.

Even thus is the task of Man, the Social Mechanic.

Our reconstructive effort must be so to reconstruct or rearrange the social mechanism as to utilize the unchangeable instincts, the economic traits (that is, the natural forces in our problem) for the accomplishment of a united social purpose, a National Objective.

Man a Spiritual Entity.

I have spoken so much in terms of mechanics that it may not be amiss to guard here against the imputation that I conceive of human life in such terms. My conception is indeed the very opposite of that. Man (though functioning in a mechanistic world through a bodily machine) is above all a spiritual entity; and his material and mechanical concerns and affairs are of importance only in so far as they affect his spiritual being.

"Society."

To avoid misunderstanding, it should be borne in mind that "Society" as used herein means the total of all those constituting the Nation—"tinker, tailor, soldier, sailor, rich man, poor man, beggarman, thief", et al.; but that Social Functioning includes only a limited part of their life in its totality.

Social functioning is the service part of modern collective (gregarious) life —for material well-being. Its relation to national life is analogous to that which the kitchen and service part in a well ordered household bears to the life of the family.

And, national economics is merely household economics expanded.

"Society" a Machine.

This is not the place for expounding at length my social philosophy. But it will suffice, as a guiding thread, to indicate that my conception of Society is the corollary of my conception of Man.

That is, I view society as a mechanical contrivance for the satisfaction of man's material needs; for the ulterior object of freeing his spiritual self. What ministers directly to his spiritual wants and his spiritual life itself, lies as clearly outside of the social organization, as outside the machine-shop.

It is in this sense also that I hold that man does not exist for society (as certain ardent social reformers would have us imagine), but society for man.

Within this frame, society resolves itself, structurally and functionally, into Production, Distribution, and Direction.

Production.

Under the term Production or Productive Group is implied that part of the community which skillfully deals with nature's forces and materials; which familiarizes itself with all matters relating to the physical environment of the human aggregation. Its function is to extract, produce and arrange all things and physical conditions desirable and necessary to the well-being of the organization.

Skilful-Strong.

Its membership is characterized by skill and strength, by curiosity rationalized into desire to know, and by a beaver-like urge—the instinct to make.

This group is not the representative of the community, nor is its function that of guardian, custodian, organizer, supervisor, or unifier of the composite group, nor has it rightly any of these functions. This Productive Group is the transforming element of the Social Machine.

"Labor."

The Labor Element we find in practice also assumes the functions of the Directive and Distributive Groups in many ways and details. And attempting to perform these functions so foreign to its character, specialized aptitude, and economic trait, it does much harm and adds misdirected energy to existing confusion.

Taking into consideration, however, the history of this group—its age-long grinding between the upper and nether millstones of Cunning-Strong and Tricksy-Cunning—the wonder is, not that the results are as they are, but rather that this group still persists in its efforts to perform any of its rightful functions, and that it has not

long ago by the misdirection of its energy wrecked the whole structure; as it has often, seemingly, been on the ragged edge of doing. Were it not for its ineradicable instinctive urge, this doubtless would have been the result.

It is not without significance that the Distributive Group is satisfied with present conventions and desperately fears change, while the Productive Group is fiercely dissatisfied, and welcomes any change.

"Efficiency."

"Production" has been of late very much to the fore in the public prints. The whole civilized world, our own country included, we are told, is not producing enough. Production, we are told, must be increased by greater industry and "efficiency."

As an inventor, that is one engaged in devising ways and means for doing something in a new and better way, I may be credited with having a sufficiently high regard for efficiency. Yet I own that, as currently conceived and employed, "efficiency" is my pet aversion. Nothing provokes me to more laughter or anger.

A notion of efficiency that focuses on the product, instead of the producer, misses the point completely. Such "efficiency" is really (humanly and socially) inefficiency.

Therefore, when I outline the task of social reconstruction as an appropriate organization of production, distribution, and direction, there are to be constantly held in mind and applied the ultimate criteria: a free unfolding of the spirit, a free manhood, a free nation.

Distribution.

Under the term Distribution or Distributive Group are implied those individuals whose function in the social organization is to keep tally and effect the distribution of products and wealth equitably and impartially to all the individuals of all the groups in accordance with their effectiveness and the best interests of the community at large.

A truly magnificent function!

Capitalist.

The "Capitalist Element" in practice, as the "Money Power" or "the

Interests", interferes most energetically and unjustifiably in matters wholly outside its sphere.

It has, in fact, assumed, through its taxing power, the functions of "Government" and control over the life and activities of every individual in the community. It has missed its way and is more distorted (if such be possible) than either of the other groups. To it is attributable in greater measure the social disturbance and confusion at present existing.

This group is characterized by an economic trait due to its (Tricksy-Cunning) origin—its members have an inherent parasitic tendency and a bee-like hoarding urge—the instinct to take.

Tally.

This group is not the community's representative any more than is the Productive group; it is not the guardian or unifier; nor has it any of the functions of government, though it has assumed many of them. Neither does it deal with nature's forces or materials; it has no concern with physical environment or natural resources; it does not extract or produce things from nature's stores; it does not make, produce, or create wealth; its functions are neither governmental nor productive in any sense.

It is simply the bookkeeper, the clerk, of the community—the recording or tabulating element of the social machine.

Tricksy-Cunning.

And yet it has arranged conventions of distribution for its own exclusive benefit.

It has appointed itself an unofficial and irresponsible custodian of the community's wealth in process of distribution. Out of the community's wealth flowing through its channels, it pays itself such wages as it deems its due for performing these services and functions. In addition to this, it retains possession of various forms of conventional increment accruing to the flowing wealth during the distributive process. These increments are deemed, by tacit acceptance of conventions made by the Distributive Group, to be its property. So this acquisitive group acts as distributive agent for producer and the community, and custodian of the products, while at the same time it is active as an untrammeled trader on its own behalf in and with the community's wealth.

Direction.

By the terms Direction or Directive Group is implied that part of the nation which neither produces nor distributes, but represents the whole composite group, the community.

It is that part which, as representative, is guardian, supervisor, and unifier. Its function is to facilitate the correct working of all the ramifying parts of the other elements, so as to bring about harmonious co-action of the entire social organization. It is the "governor" or strain and speed equalizer of the social machine.

Government.

The "Government", in practice, exercises all these social functions inextricably tangled up with the productive and distributive elements in most of their details.

Government makes, manufactures, and exploits; it keeps tally of products and distributes them more or less ineffectively; and while remaining Government in name, it performs all these other functions to such an extent that it is difficult to determine which most definitely characterizes it in reality.

This confusion of function seems to be the logical outcome of the (Cunning-Strong) genesis of the group, with its inherent lust for power and dominion—the instinct to control.

Social Mechanic's Task.

What then is the task of Man, the Social Mechanic?

Primarily, it is to extricate the basic three-fold elements of the social mechanism from the present confusion and distortion; and, in the light of and under the guidance of Science, so to organize these fundamental functions: Production, Distribution, and Direction, that they will serve the social purpose, the national objective.

What the Trouble Is.

As it stands now, the Social Machine is a product of nature-made conditions, and not a construction of self-conscious human intelligence directed to the accomplishment of a predetermined human purpose.

Man has never attempted to organize his Social Machinery to accomplish a socially unified object. And Nature does not stop, simply because man acts like a fool. Nature truly abhors a vacuum—especially a vacuity of intelligence.

Man has tinkered with many social details—he has never tackled the Social Problem!

That is the whole trouble with the Social Machine.

Social Problem

The situation is not unlike that of a machine-shop in which a lot of mentally deranged mechanics would find themselves while gradually and unequally convalescing toward rationality.

They find the engine and machinery (Nature) all running smoothly, but also they find themselves (with more or less bewilderment) individually and in bunches, marvelously and solemnly busy doing, with great skill, all manner of grotesque stunts: stoking the furnaces with their women and children, feeding their young men to the ponderous grinding and crushing machines; tirelessly dumping the most valued and useful products of their bodies, brains, and skill, to the smashing "dead-falls" and scrapping "go-devils", to be crushed to human slimes and refuse; and in a multitude of other ways ingeniously employing their (Nature-made) facilities and capabilities to produce all kinds of silly outcomes—unlikable to their awakening intelligence.

The condition thus disclosed they call their "Social Problem".

Man Is Free.

Man has a living Godlike soul which is free. As a "person"—a spiritual entity—a Man is not a machine, is not subject to control by any power in the Universe except himself, and except in so far as—by an exercise of his freedom—he voluntarily submits.

In so far as he does submit to force or irrational control, he becomes a mere product—a machine; he contracts his own soul and diminishes that transcendent quality of Godship which makes him a Man—his Freedom.

A Purposive Social Machine.

I firmly believe that Man is, and the Universe is, so constituted that Human Intelligence can construct a Rational Social Machine; that if Man earnestly desires and has the courage seriously to undertake the task, he can make an infinitely more smooth-running, humanly efficient, and humanly purposive arrangement than the humanly objectless, inhumanly cruel, and incredibly wasteful Stone Age animalistic abortion to which he now submits—that Man can make a Social Machine worthy of Man, the World Mechanic.

Human Intelligence or Animal Instincts?

"Nature", while on one hand seemingly reckless of "waste", is on the other obviously economical—structures, functions, and "gifts" not used, atrophy and disappear.

If then Man, in social relation, fails to use his "gifts", these will atrophy—be recalled. And Man's social development will run not in accord with his intelligence, but in accord with his animal instincts, dominated by the most basic of all, the anti-social (individual) self-preservation instinct—dog-eat-dog—jungle law.

Science a Fulcrum.

It may seem that I have made of the existing social disorder an arraignment of Man's competence. I have charged him with folly, with failure to use his greatest gifts: reason and freedom.

Perhaps he can bring forward extenuations. Perhaps the time had not come—till now.

Perhaps there has been neither lack of human intelligence nor lack of willingness to use it. Perhaps he really could not use it, did not know how

For one thing he lacked, which has come only in our own day: Experimental Science.

Science is a firm fulcrum for the lever of thought.

It is a fulcrum securely resting upon the eternal facts and laws of nature.

It is a fulcrum that rests upon phenomenal truth, which rests upon Nature's immanent Essential Truth that makes for universal right-eousness—mechanistic validity, personal worth, social right.

Technocracy.

The philosophers and thinkers of the past lacked that fulcrum. At the best, they could be only good guessers. There is no lack of intelligence or high spirituality in Plato's "Republic", in More's "Utopia", and in their many followers.

But they all lacked, and all they

lacked was, the firm fulcrum of Science.

This we now possess.

Now only has Technocracy become a realizable ideal.

This transcendent acquisition and necessary instrumentality—Science—is now ours to freely use or freely abuse—abuse to our irrecoverable hurt or utilize for our ever increasing and true prosperity.

This is our signal acquisition as compared with the past, our significant point of progress. And by its aid (if we choose) we (socially still in the pre-scientific period) may at last achieve also social progress.

And thus, by the means of nationally organized Science, we may become the first real nation, a truly united people with a worth-while national objective—a true Industrial Democracy—an intelligently purposeful TECHNOCRACY.

Fernwald, Berkeley, California.
November 21, 1920.

CAN MODERN MECHANIZED SOCIETY SAFELY RELY UPON TRADITIONAL ECONOMIC CUSTOMS?